Invitation to Go

Preface

GO IS FUN

This game of simple rules has already been developed over hundreds of years into perhaps the most stimulating and subtle battle of wits in the world of games. Yet in spite of its high degree of development, because of its simplicity of form you can impose *your* will, *your* personality on the game.

Go is for everyone

Judgement and experience are at least as important in Go as mental agility, and young and old are equally represented at even the highest and most strenuous levels of the game.

Go has a past, a present, and a future

You can relax by browsing through the games and lore of Go-players of centuries past or you can join in the energetic bustle of tournaments and clubs, confident in the knowledge that the computer is not going to take over in the foreseeable future.

In short, Go offers you a lifetime of pleasure. This book introduces you to the way we play Go in the West today with the hope that it can adequately mirror the fascination of this great game.

John Fairbairn

ACKNOWLEDGEMENTS

I enjoyed writing this book. The main reason for this was the unstinting help readily and cheerfully given by the many people I turned to. In particular I must thank Tom McDonald of the Edinburgh Go club, who supplied the original drawing for the cover; Stuart Dowsey and his staff at the London Go Centre; and Jim Bates of London. The photograph on page 4 was kindly provided by Christine Knight through Knight Games of London and the photograph on page 77 by Nigel Sutton of the Hampstead and Highgate Express.

Contents

1 *It's so easy to start*

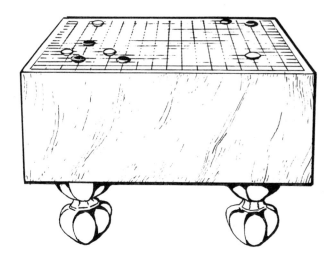

All you need to play Go are
> two players
> a board
> a set of stones
> about ½ to 1½ hours for a friendly game

THE PLAYERS
One of the best features of Go is that any two players of equal or unequal
strength can play a rewarding game.

THE BOARD
Rich players, or masochists who like to sit with their legs folded under
them, may like to buy the elegant kind of Go board shown above. Most
people, however, make do with a flat board of wood, metal, or cardboard,
on which is marked a grid of 19 × 19 lines. The dimensions of a standard
board are
> playing grid   381 × 423 mm (line separation 21 and 23·5 mm)
> actual board 406 × 450 × 20 mm.
This size is correct for the standard stones.
   The board is longer in the direction between the two players to allow for

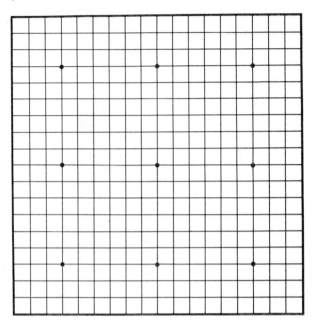

Diagram 1   The Go Board

perspective. You will see nine small dots marked at certain intersections (one at the centre, the rest on the fourth line from the edge). These are the 'star points', and are used only in handicapping.

Some beginners prefer to play on smaller boards, usually of 13 × 13 or 9 × 9 lines. This has no effect on any of the rules.

THE STONES

The circular black and white pieces used in Go are called stones, a term borrowed from the Japanese. In expensive sets the black stones are made of slate and the white of clam shell, but plastic is now the most common material. A standard set contains 181 black stones and 180 white, although the exact number is not important.

If you prefer to make your own stones, as many have done before (with buttons, Smarties, drawing pins, etc — my own first set used tiddleywinks), or when you buy a set, remember that the stones should just touch when they are placed on adjacent intersections.

It is helpful to keep the stones in containers with lids, one for the black stones and one for the white. Wooden bowls designed specially for Go stones are available, at prices ranging from the reasonable to the ridiculous.

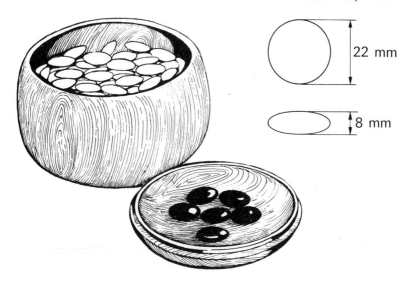

22 mm

8 mm

GRADES

Amateur players are graded by using a *dan* and *kyu* system, as in Judo. A complete beginner is somewhere around 30-kyu. If he improves sufficiently he can rise to 1-kyu. The dan grades represent the next stage up, but (in contrast to the kyus) the dans start at 1 for the lowest and only go up to 6. 1-dan is usually referred to as *sho-dan* (beginning dan).

You can get a kyu grade by playing someone of known grading. Promotion is then a matter of what you want to call yourself, but if you join a club the secretary will probably regulate promotions to help keep a uniform national standard. Promotion to and in the dan grades is strictly controlled by national associations.

Professionals have their own grading system, starting with sho-dan (equivalent to a 7-dan amateur) and going up to 9-dan.

There are no belts corresponding to gr es, as in Judo – just diplomas for dan players. The grades are used ma   to fix handicaps between players of different strengths and it is   ays good to have a yardstick like this to gauge your own improvement.

CONVENTIONS

The 'plonk'. This has nothing to do with the rules, or skill; but it is the done thing in Go to plonk the stones firmly down on the board. You should hold the stone between the tips of the first two fingers, as shown in

3

the photograph. As you touch the board withdraw your bottom finger; then slide the stone into the proper position.

The plonk is supposed to show resolution and determination in the face of the enemy's onslaught. (In practice the effect is often to scatter the stones already on the board all over the floor.) Nothing brands a player as a beginner more than his plonk, or lack of it.

As a matter of fact the quality of connoisseurs' Go boards is assessed partly by the pleasantness of the sound they make when plonked upon.

It is also a convention for the first player to make the first move in his top right-hand corner. This is not a rule, and you will, for instance, also see first moves played at the centre point, or on the sides.

Apart from this there is no rigmarole to go through such as bowing, or screams of *kyaaa*!!, which may prevail in other forms of leisure borrowed from the East. All you need now is a few rules. And here is another of the excellent features of Go: few rules.

2 The rules, and the object of the game

You will find it easy to learn the basic rules of Go but then if you are not careful problems will arise.

You may be confused first of all by the very size of the Go board. Secondly you may be confused by playing with a stronger player who can manipulate the exceptions called *ko* and *seki* to his advantage and make them seem harder than they really are.

I therefore recommend you to start playing on a smaller board, preferably 13×13 lines, and to avoid stronger players like the plague until you have sorted out the rules and their implications in your own mind first. Some people don't agree with this and, indeed, when I started I thought it was sacrilege not to play on the full board, but most of the experienced teachers of Go in the West would agree with the advice given here. 13×13 boards are ideal because they allow virtually the same strategy as is possible on the 19×19 board.

THE MOVES

Play starts with the board empty. The weaker player takes the black stones and plays first. Moves are then played alternately.

A move consists of taking a stone from your own bowl and placing it on any vacant intersection (*not* in a square), subject to two prohibitions described below. Once a stone has been played it is never moved unless it is captured by the opponent, in which case he simply removes it. Since captures are relatively infrequent the board gradually fills up with stones as the game proceeds.

Black plays first, but if he receives a handicap (see later for details) he places between 2 and 9 stones on the star points, and this counts as his first move. If both players are of equal strength the way Go players usually decide who takes Black is for one to take a handful of stones and the other to guess whether the number he holds is odd or even. If he is right he takes Black. This process is called *nigiri*.

THE OBJECT OF THE GAME

The object is to form continuous lines, or *walls*, of your own stones, so as to surround vacant areas of the board. Every *vacant* intersection inside such 'territories' counts one point for the owner, if he still controls this territory at the end of the game. (If he loses the territory he loses the points.)

You may also capture your opponent's stones, and you score one point for each stone you capture during the game. Since the captured stone is

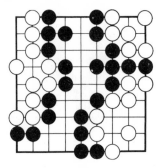

Diagram 2 Territory

removed it vacates a point of territory. If you still control this territory at the end of the game you will count this point too. Each captured stone counts one point, even if you eventually lose the territory it came from.

The player with the most points at the end of the game is the winner.

Diagram 2 shows you on a 9×9 board what territory looks like at the end of a game. Remembering that only vacant intersections count, White has 2 points in the top right-hand corner, 8 points in the bottom right, and 6 points along the left edge, a total of 16 points.

Black has only one territory, but this is worth 18 points; so Black would win this game by 2 points, assuming there were no captured pieces.

There is no significance in the size of a victory, except that if it is consistently large the handicaps need to be adjusted.

You will note in this example that the walls are by no means straight. This is of course the result of having to adapt to the opponent's plays. Another thing to note is that the edge of the board acts as a natural boundary for either player.

LIBERTIES

A liberty is a vacant intersection immediately adjacent to a stone *along one of the lines marked on the board.* Single stones normally have four liberties (Diagram 3A), but stones on the edge have only three, and in the corner there are only two possible liberties. The points marked *x* in the diagram are the liberties for those stones. Remember the intersection must be vacant to count as a liberty.

The same principle applies to groups. The group in Diagram 3B has liberties at the points marked *x*.

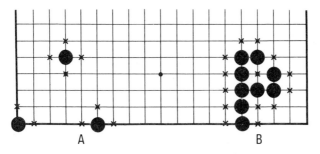

Diagram 3   Liberties

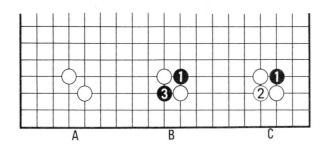

Diagram 4   White 2 elsewhere

CONNECTED STONES

If a stone is placed on one of the liberties of a stone of the same colour the two are said to be *solidly connected*. They then contribute liberties to each other. You can see this in Diagram 3B. Once stones are solidly connected the connection can never be broken.

The two stones in Diagram 4A look connected but aren't. Black can play at 1 and, if White does not answer, at 3 (Diagram 4B) to separate them completely. In 4C, however, White 2 answers Black 1, and now the white stones are solidly connected.

CAPTURING

If a player occupies with his own stones *all* the liberties of one of his opponent's stones or groups of stones he captures the surrounded pieces, and takes them off the board. He should put them in the lid of his bowl, so that he will remember to count them at the end of the game. (Incidentally either player is entitled to know at any time how many of his stones have been captured.)

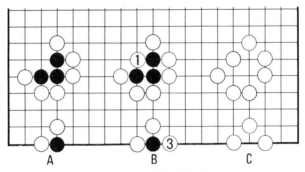

Diagram 5 Capture Black 2 elsewhere

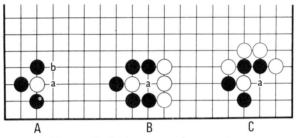

Diagram 6 Saving stones from capture

At the bottom of Diagram 5A Black has one stone with one liberty. At
the top he has a group of three stones, also with only one liberty left among
them. In both cases the black stones are in a position of capture. They are
said to be in *atari*. If White wants to capture them (and Black does not stop
him) he plays at 1 and 3 to fill in the last liberties (5B). The board will then
look as in 5C, because White takes off any stones he captures.

If your stones are threatened with capture and you want to save them
you can do one of three things, each illustrated in Diagram 6. In each case
a white stone is in atari, and Black could capture it by playing at *a*. However, if White plays at *a* first he will save his stone.

A. He can add a stone to provide the threatened stone with more liberties.
The connection must be solid. If White plays at *b* instead Black can still
play at *a* to capture the single stone.

B. Here White can join it up to an existing group. Again the connection
must be solid.

C. Finally he may be able to capture part of the surrounding wall. When
White plays at *a* here he is capturing two black stones. When he removes
these he is giving his own stones more liberties.

8

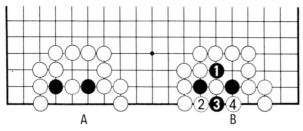

Diagram 7   Dead stones

DEAD STONES

If a group or a single stone is surrounded by enemy stones in such a way that it cannot avoid capture (even though it may have several liberties), it is said to be dead. *At the end of the game* the player surrounding a dead group removes these stones as if they had been captured. He counts one point for each of these prisoners, and also of course one point for each vacant point of territory exposed when they are removed. He does not actually have to fill in all the dead group's liberties with his own stones.

The reason for not removing them until the end of the game is that dead stones have many uses while they are on the board, for instance in ko fights. They may also come back to life if, for instance, part of the surrounding wall is captured.

Diagram 7A shows two dead black stones. If this were the end of the game they would just be removed and no other stones added. Diagram 7B shows Black trying in vain to avoid capture. White 2 captures the Black stone on the left, and White 4 captures Black 3. Your immediate reaction may be that there are cases when it is hard to tell whether stones can avoid capture or not. True — this is part and parcel of the tactics of the game.

You should note that stones are dead only if both players regard them as such. Their owner is quite entitled to try and save them, even if he is wasting his time.

PROHIBITED MOVES

There are two rules prohibiting certain moves: the 'Suicide Rule' and the 'Rule of Ko'.

The Suicide Rule

Despite the Oriental predilection for suicide it is not permitted in Go. The rule therefore forbids you to make any move that would leave one of your stones or groups without any liberties. In other words you must not 'commit suicide' by playing into a position of capture.

The rules, and the object of the game

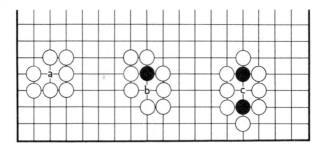

Diagram 8

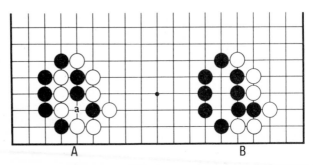

Diagram 9

In Diagram 8 Black is not allowed to play at *a, b*, or *c*, because his stone or group would then have no liberties.

There is, however, one very important exception to this rule. A stone may be played into a position of capture *if in doing so it captures any of the opponent's stones*. Black is thus allowed to play at *a* in Diagram 9A, even though his right-hand group then has no liberties, because this move captures some white stones. The resulting position in 9B shows you why — when the captured white stones have been removed the black stones have plenty of liberties. Note that if it were White's move in A he could also play at *a* and capture three black stones.

The Rule of Ko
Ko is a Japanese word meaning 'eternity'. In Go it refers to a position which is continually repeated, and would go on for ever unless something were done to stop it.

The rule therefore forbids any move that would leave the position identical to the position before the move the opponent has just made. Thus

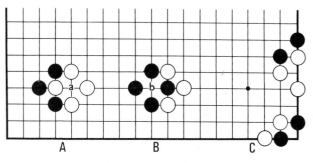

Diagram 10   Ko

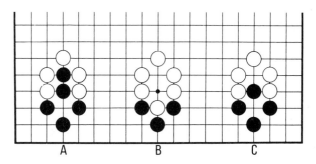

Diagram 11   Not ko

in Diagram 10A Black can capture one white stone by playing at *a*. (Remember that this is not suicide because he is capturing.) In the resulting position (10B) Black's capturing stone is itself in atari. If White were now to play at *b* and capture this stone we should be back to the situation in A. This sequence could go on for ever, except that the rule makes it illegal to capture straight back in a ko. Instead you must make a move elsewhere first, giving your opponent an opportunity to resolve the ko situation (e.g. Black can play at *b* in 10B.) If he doesn't take this opportunity then you can play back in the ko, because with the moves just made the position can no longer be identical.

All ko situations (or 'ko fights'), irrespective of how confusing the surrounding position may be, involve one of the three positions shown in 10A and 10C, the two positions in 10C being, of course, variations of that in 10A.

The position in Diagram 11 is not ko. If in A White takes the two black stones in atari, leaving the position as in B, Black can retake the one white stone immediately (C) because this situation is not repetitive.

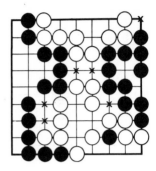

Diagram 12   Dame

THE END OF THE GAME

The game ends when both players agree that no more useful plays can be made; i.e. no more territory can be made or defended; no more captures can be made or prevented.

The territories of both players are then counted and totalled, the number of captured pieces being added to the respective totals.

After most games you will find that there are vacant points on the board that do not belong to either player's territory—points like those marked *x* in Diagram 12, which lie in a kind of no-man's land between opposing walls. Neither player can completely surround these points, and it is of no advantage to either player to occupy them. Neither player can count them as part of his territory.

These points are called neutral points, or more commonly by the Japanese name *dame* (rhymes with macramé). Dame are of no particular significance, but when the game is finished there is the danger that one player might accidentally count them as part of his territory. For this reason, before counting begins, it is usual to fill up all these neutral points with spare stones (*not* with your captured stones!). It normally makes no difference who fills them in, or in what order.

Strictly speaking a game ends when one player says 'Pass', and then the other player passes. Actually we rarely bother with this and the usual way for a game to end is for one player to say something like, 'Okay, let's fill in the dame'.

If both players do not agree that the game is over the safest course is to continue playing until agreement is reached. If this happens to you and you can't see any reason for playing on, don't. If you put a stone in your own territory just for the sake of playing on you are taking away one of your own points. If you put a stone in one of your opponent's territories you are giving him one point extra for a dead stone.

You can fill in a dame, or you can pass if you prefer, but if you have passed your opponent is then entitled to play. You can keep passing, but at any time you can intervene to answer your opponent's moves. If you have made the right decision your opponent is wasting his time and yours (he may also be throwing away stones inside your territory, which will please you). If you haven't, you may find for instance that your opponent has managed to cut off some of your stones and capture them, or even to form a live (uncapturable) group inside one of your territories. If this does happen don't cry; it's happened to all of us.

You may of course resign at any time during the game if you are losing by too large a margin to catch up (say 10–20 points). There is no special way of doing this, except perhaps gracefully.

3 Territory! Territory! Territory!

Go is not really a war game—it is a game of coexistence. It is not unusual to go through an entire game without capturing a single stone, but many players forget that the object of the game is to surround territory, and they try instead to capture the opponent's stones. When the fight is over they look at the board and find that by pure chance they have surrounded a few little pieces of territory here and there.

One problem with territory, however, is keeping hold of it. After a few games against a stronger player in which he overruns every area of territory you thought was safely yours, you start wondering whether you've understood the rules or not. In fact the concept of *secure* territory is a difficult one, and worth spending a little time on.

TWO EYES

The first requirement for a secure territory is that the wall surrounding it should be safe from capture.

In Diagram 13, White can capture the black group on the left by just playing at *a*. This black territory is far from secure.

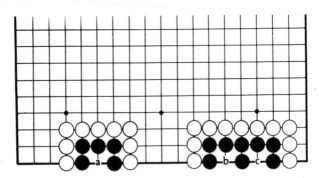

Diagram 13

To capture the black group on the right, however, White needs to play at both *b* and *c*. He cannot play two moves simultaneously, but neither can he play here in two consecutive moves. The reason is that a play at either point is suicide. White can only play a suicidal move if in the process he captures the black group. He cannot capture this black group, because he first has to fill in the other liberty, which is impossible.

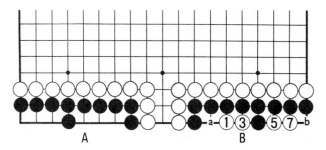

Diagram 14 Safe against all attacks   Black 2,4,6 elsewhere

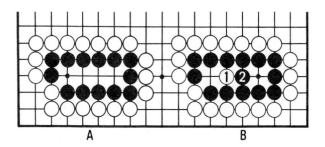

Diagram 15 Safe but must defend

The same applies in Diagram 14: the black group at A is completely
safe. If White tries to capture, Black doesn't even have to answer. In B
White has had four free moves, but he still cannot capture Black because
he is still unable to play at *a* and *b* simultaneously.

This principle obviously applies to larger territories too. When a group is
safe from capture it is said to be *alive* or to have *two eyes*. As you saw above
the feature that ensured the life, or safety, of the black groups was that they
had *two* separate spaces within them which White could not fill simultaneously, and he couldn't fill each one in turn because this would have been
suicide for his stones. These two separate spaces are the 'two eyes'. An eye
is a space that may contain any number of points, so be careful not to con-
fuse eyes and points.

It is not always necessary actually to form the two eyes to ensure the
safety of a group. In Diagram 15A the black group is safe. You can see why
in 15B. If White plays 1, Black plays 2. If White 2, then Black 1. Alive!
Note that Black's original group (in 15A) is quite safe, and he should not
waste points and moves forming the two eyes unless he is forced to do so
by White. What might happen if Black does not respond to the threat is
shown in Diagrams 44—47 and 68—73.

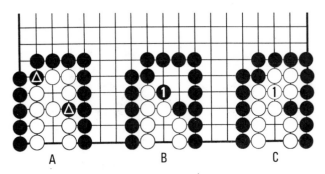

Diagram 16 False eyes

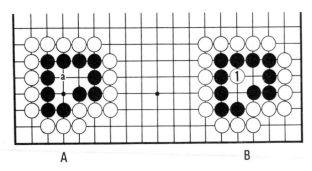

Diagram 17 Life or death depends on who plays first

FALSE EYES

A frequent trap for players of all levels is to make *false eyes*. These are spaces which look like eyes but aren't, because they have to be filled in. Diagram 16A shows a typical example. White does seem to have two eyes, but one is false. Which one?

The one at the top is false, because if it is Black's move he can capture the three stones, removing them and the eye (Diagram B). If it is White's move in A he can defend his three stones by connecting them to the main group (Diagram C), but this also leaves him with only one eye. To make two eyes White needed a stone at one of the points ⬤ in Diagram A.

One eye, unless it is big enough to split into two eyes when under attack, does not ensure the life of a group.

The black group in Diagram 17A has one eye at the moment. Black *a* would ensure two eyes and life, but if White gets to play at *a* first (Diagram B) he kills Black. However Black plays, now White can capture the whole black group. Try the various move-orders yourself.

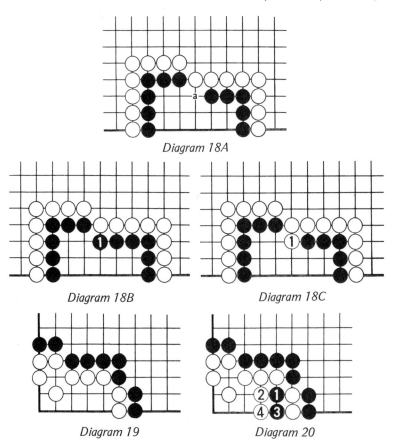

Diagram 18A

Diagram 18B   *Diagram 18C*

Diagram 19   *Diagram 20*

INVASION FROM OUTSIDE

To be quite secure, territory must be *completely surrounded*, so that it is safe against invasion from the outside. There is a gap in the wall surrounding Black's territory at *a* in Diagram 18A. If Black can play here his territory will be safe (B). If White plays here (C) Black's territory is destroyed.

There must be *no defects* in the surrounding wall if the territory is to be secure. White's territory in Diagram 19 looks safe, because there are no gaps in the surrounding wall, but there is a defect which Black can exploit to reduce the size of this territory. Can you find it?

The answer is shown in Diagram 20. Black 1 and 3 capture two white stones. White 2 and 4 make his territory secure, but four points smaller than he thought it was. Note here, as in many other examples, how the edge of the board plays an important role in capturing stones.

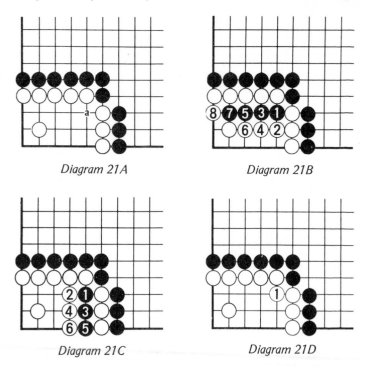

Diagram 21A

Diagram 21B

Diagram 21C

Diagram 21D

Often a wall seems to have a defect although it is really quite sound. At first glance the wall in Diagram 21A seems to have (at *a*) the same defect as in Diagram 19. This time, however, White can easily capture the invading stones, provided he plays correctly, as in B. If White plays the other way (as in C), he does lose a sizeable chunk of his territory, for part of his wall is captured.

If you are faced with a situation like the one in Diagram 21A and you are not sure whether or not the wall is safe you may prefer to add an extra stone such as White 1 in D to patch up the weakness. Notice that by doing this you are depriving yourself of one point of territory, as well as foregoing the chance to play at a more important part of the board. Safety-first play has much to recommend it for beginners, but you should try, as you become more experienced, to dispense with moves like these which are not strictly necessary.

INVASION FROM INSIDE

White has played inside Black's territory in Diagram 22. (At times like this one feels a distinct antipathy towards one's opponent.) Either Black has

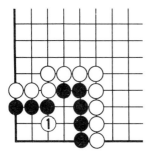

Diagram 22   The vital point

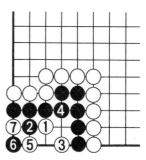

Diagram 23   Ko

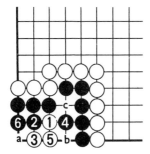

Diagram 24   Seki

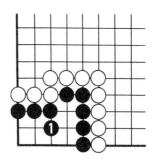

Diagram 25   Alive

made his territory too big (or the wrong shape), or he can capture the invading stone(s).

In such cases the invader again tries to exploit defects in the surrounding wall. He can try to capture the wall, perhaps by ko, or to live, by two eyes or *seki*.

In Diagram 23 he has made a ko. If he wins this ko he can capture the wall.

Seki

In Diagram 24 White is alive simply because Black can't kill him. If Black *a* or *b*, White *c* captures one black group. But White can't kill Black either: if White *a*, Black *b*; or if White *b*, Black *a*. This stalemate position is called *seki*, and is fairly common. The ruling is that *no points are counted in a seki*, for either player, and both groups are regarded as alive. More details of sekis are given in Chapter 8.

If Black had played 1 first, as in Diagram 25, White would be wasting his time invading. In fact if White plays anywhere here Black can ignore it and White has thus given away one point for an unnecessary dead stone.

4 The Grand Final

Join us if you will for the tense closing moments of the Lower Greenwich Newcomers Knockout Final. In the far corner of the cramped L-shaped room above the bar that the local Go enthusiasts call home two players sit locked in gladiatorial combat, while around them, gazing with Zeus-like solemnity at the play of mere mortals, cluster the spectators, attracted like vultures to the kill.

It looks as if Ernest is going to win. Ernest is a precocious teenager who only learnt the game a week ago. Except for his rapid improvement the other Go players find him utterly likeable; so it will be a popular victory.

Opposite him sits Sammy Swindler (there's one in every club). Basically Sammy is one of life's born losers. The problem is not so much that he's dim, although that has been said. It's really that he doesn't know how to make life go his way. Once in a while he beats even the best players in the club, but instead of getting the credit he manages to be branded as 'lucky'. Perhaps it would help if he made more moves based on thought rather than pure optimism.

The game in fact has come to an end. Ernest, inwardly terrified that Sammy might disagree and play on to try and devastate one of his territories, has suggested that they should count up. Fortunately Sammy agrees, and counting begins. Ernest is disconcerted to find that Sammy is retrieving captured pieces not only from the lid of his bowl, but also off the floor, from inside a beer glass, and from other places that only Sammy would think of. Ernest hasn't been at the club long enough to learn his opponent's ways, and the sudden reappearance of captured stones has upset his calculations considerably. So much so in fact that when all is done the unbelievable has happened, and Sammy Swindler has won.

The game is recorded on the following pages. Strategically it is an awful game, but it has one great advantage: it illustrates almost all the rules of Go.

Sammy has Black and they are playing on a 13 × 13 board.

Diagram 26 (moves 1—12)
This is the way Go games are given in books (even Japanese books; so you can read them too!). It looks easy to follow games just by reading the diagrams, but it isn't. It is far better to play games out on a board.

The next move is sometimes hard to find in these diagrams. This problem disappears as you gain experience, since then you can usually guess whereabouts the next move should be. Sometimes, though, a move cannot be put on a diagram for some reason—look beside or below the diagram and

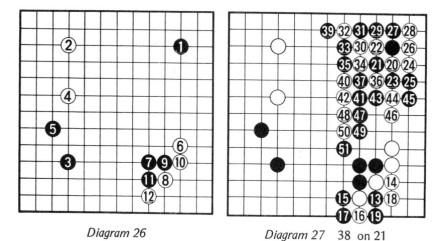

Diagram 26   Diagram 27   <u>38</u> on 21

you'll find it there. If a move is underlined on the board there is a comment about it in the text.

Black 1: This is easy to find, because it follows the convention of playing in the top right corner. Opening moves *should* be played at strategic points, to map out prospective territories; but our two players find this hard to believe, and their opening moves are just a way of filling in time before the middle game starts.

White 12: White plans to start sealing off the territory in the corner, expecting Black to play to the left of 12. However, this white stone is not solidly connected to the one at 8 . . .

Diagram 27 (13–51)

. . . and so Black cuts it off.

Black 13: This first of all attacks the white stone above (at 8) by filling in one of its two remaining liberties. It is now in atari; so White defends by connecting it to his stones on the right.

Black 15: Again Black puts a white stone in atari, and this time White cannot save it. That doesn't stop him trying. After the inevitable sequence, up to Black 19, Black captures two white stones instead of one. He removes these two stones at once and puts them in his lid.

White 20: Stung by his mistake in the bottom corner, White turns his attention elsewhere. This is another good feature of Go: a mistake in one part of the board does not necessarily mean the end of the game, because there is usually room to make profit somewhere else.

From this point a dogfight begins. In the excitement, and no doubt spurred on by the lust to kill, both players forget entirely about forming territory and just concentrate on killing each other's groups. This is a common fault right up to 1-kyu and beyond.

On first reflection, since you get a possible two points for capturing a stone (one for the prisoner plus maybe another point for the territory underneath) you might think it best to concentrate on capturing. The trouble is that your opponent might get two eyes for his attacked group, in which case your moves would be wasted. Moreover he could then attack you almost without risk if his group were safe. Apart from anything else, though, it is easier to make territory.

White 22 separates Black's two stones, but White 20 and 22 are also separated. This means that both players have two groups to look after here. They will try to strengthen their own groups by attacking the enemy.

Black 23 puts White 20 in atari, which is why White plays at 24. Black 25 threatens to capture White's two stones by playing at 26. Then, as in the bottom corner, White would not be able to escape because he would run into the edge of the board.

Black 29, like Black 33, White 34, and Black 35, puts one stone (or group) in atari. White 36, however, captures, and removes, one stone (Black 21). Black 37 threatens to capture three white stones (22, 30, and 34) by playing at 21, since this is the ore remaining liberty of that group. White plays here first, however, with move 38, and so joins this group to the group on the right which still has several liberties.

There are two points to note here. One is that White 38 cannot be put on the diagram, because stone 21 is already recorded there, and the other is that Black would have been allowed to play at the point vacated by 21 because this would have captured three white stones and would not therefore have been suicide.

Black 39 and White 40 are atari moves.

Black 47 is to save the three black stones above: a white play here would ensure their capture next move. White continues to chase this group with 48 and 50.

After Black 51 Black's fleeing stones are now safely connected to the lower group. It is not a solid connection, but if White tries to cut Black off with a play to the right of 51 Black will just capture the white stone next move. So White now tries something else.

Diagram 28 (52—82)

Note in this diagram that the captured stones 12, 16, and 21, having been removed, are no longer shown.

White 52: Atari on two stones. Black then captures the white stone at 32 but White 54 puts the same two stones back into atari. Black 55 connects

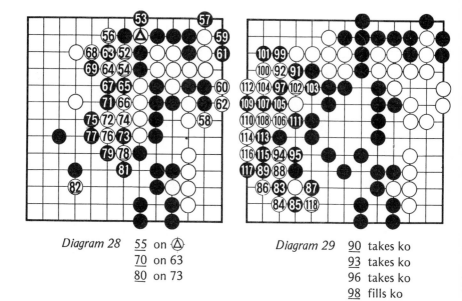

Diagram 28 55 on ⓐ
70 on 63
80 on 73

Diagram 29 90 takes ko
93 takes ko
96 takes ko
98 fills ko

at the point vacated by White 32. After White 56 Black suddenly realizes his large group on the top edge is in danger of capture. He has no room to make two eyes on the edge (don't forget about false eyes); so his only hope is to cut off part of the surrounding wall. He tries one way with 57-61 but this fails when White 62 captures three black stones, which provides extra liberties for the corner white group that Black was attacking. Now Black switches to the other side.

White 68 captures the black stone 63. Black 69 is atari on three stones; so White plays move 70 at 63 to save them.

Black 73: Also atari, as are 75 and 77. White 78 captures one stone. Black 79 is again atari and White 80 fills at 73, but this ploy, which has worked twice for him so far, fails here. Black 81 fills in the last liberty of the group of 10 white stones and so captures them. This also saves his own group at the top. With 82 White begins an attack on the bottom left corner.

Diagram 29 (83—118)
Rather than resign White is going to try to make up for his large loss in the centre by taking the bottom left corner from Black. He already has some virtually secure territory on the right side and some prospects of territory in the top left corner. If he gets the bottom corner as well he may win. Black 87 captures one stone.

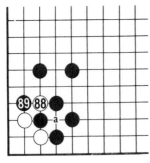

Diagram 30

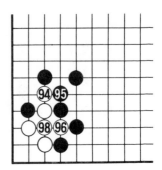

Diagram 31

Ko fight

White 90 is the start of a ko fight. The position in the bottom left-hand corner after Black 89 was as shown in Diagram 30. White 90 is played at *a*. This captures stone 83 and also relieves the atari on 88. According to the rule of ko Black cannot capture back immediately since this would be a repetitive situation. He must play elsewhere first.

If Black wants to take back the ko (and he does here, because control of the corner is vital to the result of the game) he has to find a move elsewhere that is so threatening that White must answer it. He does this by playing at 91. White answers at 92, because if he doesn't he might lose all of the top corner. This gives Black the opportunity to take the ko back, i.e. to play move 93 on the point previously occupied by 83, capturing one stone (White 90) in the process.

Now it is White who cannot capture back immediately; so he has to find a move which Black will find threatening enough to answer, which explains 94 and 95 (Black didn't like the look of a White stone at 115 if he doesn't answer). White now takes one black stone (93) in the ko.

Black 97 is another ko threat, but this time White takes a chance and ignores it. He fills in the ko — in other words plays 98 on the point vacated by Black 93. The ko is now completely finished and the situation here is as shown in Diagram 31.

White took this chance because he knew he was behind—a good decision on his part because it shows awareness of what is happening over the whole board. Players who get bogged down in one area of the board without realizing how the overall game is going will never really improve.

Black 99 is the logical continuation. White has in effect allowed Black one extra move here by filling in the ko. 99 cuts White 92 off from the group of seven stones to its right. The principle of divide and conquer applies in Go as anywhere else.

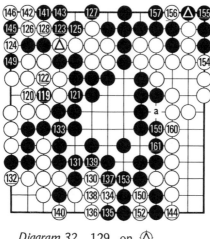

Diagram 32   129   on ⊛
               <u>147</u>   on 145
               <u>148</u>   on 126
               151   fills ko (at 124)
               158   on ⬤

White 102 to 110 are all atari. So is Black 111, but White gets out of this by capturing four black stones with 112.

Black wants to capture the white group on the left but first he has to cut it off from the white group at the bottom: hence the sequence up to 117. After this White's corner group looks very unhealthy; so he plays 118 to ensure two eyes (one in the corner and one by capturing Black 85).

Diagram 32 (119–161)
Black 119: Black is being too optimistic. White has two eyes after 122. There was no way for Black to prevent this; so there is no way he can capture White (remember he cannot commit suicide in either of White's eyes). Even without Black 119 White's group is still safe, because although he has not actually formed the two eyes, he can always form them under attack. If Black plays 119 at 120, White plays 119 and stays alive.

What about two eyes for the other groups on the board? White's big territory on the right already has two eyes. So has Black's centre group (one on the top edge, one in the middle). White's group in the bottom left has already been mentioned. That leaves the white group in the top left, but Black has plans for that.

Black 123: He is going to kill this group before it has a chance to make any eyes. With 127 he captures the seven stones. White 128 and 132 are atari, as are Black 137 and 139. White 140 captures one stone.

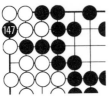

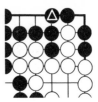

Diagram 33   Diagram 34   Diagram 35

Moves at this stage of the game are normally just to seal off the final bits of territory, but nasty things can still happen. White 144 was a good move in itself, but would have been worth more points to White at 145 in the opposite corner. Black is now able to sacrifice one stone at 145 and in return get four White stones. The technique of 145 is called a *throw-in*, and its effect, as you can see, is to make the opponent fill in his own liberties. Now Black can capture back at 147 (which is played on the same point as 145) straight away because this is not an endlessly repetitive situation; it is not ko (Diagram 33).

Black 147 also puts one white stone in atari, but instead of defending it directly White counterattacks with 148 (Diagram 34). This puts one black stone in atari, hoping to win back the corner. Black gets out of this by taking a white stone at 149 (he could also simply play at *a*), but if you look carefully you will see this is ko. White cannot play straight back; so he makes a ko threat on two black stones at 150.

Sensing that he is ahead (more advanced players actually count the game while it is in progress) Black decides to ignore White's ko threat and settles the ko by filling it (i.e. plays 151 at 124).

White 152: For peace of mind in the ko Black has had to give up the two stones that White captures with 152. This move also puts three black stones in atari.

Black 155 is a complete oversight. The four stones in the corner are not yet connected to the main group, and White 156 captures them by filling in their last liberty. It takes a long time to avoid this apparently simple kind of error. 155 should have been at 156 (⬤ in Diagram 35); this allows White to capture two stones, but then Black would capture the white stone in the corner straight back (this of course is not ko).

You will also see from this diagram that Black did not have two eyes on the edge (refer back to moves 57 and 63). If he played one point to the left of 156 he would have one eye on the left but the eye on the right is false, because either White can capture here or Black has to fill in. Either way the eye is occupied.

After Black 161 the game is finished. There is one dame (neutral point)

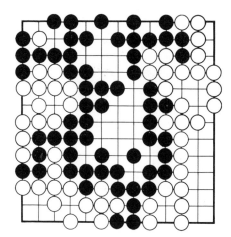

Diagram 36   Black has 21 captured pieces;
White has 27 in his lid plus
one dead stone on the board.

at *a* which White fills in. (Black could have done this: it all depends on who is feeling most lethargic.) The final position is now as in Diagram 36.

Diagram 36
There is one dead stone — the white stone in the top left corner. This is removed and put in the lid with all the other captured white stones. Counting now begins.

The procedure for simplifying the count will now be described, but to make sure that you understand it remember:

White's total number of points is the number of vacant points of territory he has surrounded at the end of the game plus *the total number of black stones he has captured (in this case 21).*

Black's total is the number of points of territory he has surrounded at the end of the game plus *the total number of white stones he has captured (28 here).*

Note: captured here includes dead stones removed.

What happens now is that each player takes the stones he has captured and places them anywhere inside the opponent's territory.

The effect of this is that you are subtracting points from yourself by getting rid of your captured stones, but at the same time you are subtracting the same number of points from your opponent by filling in his territory.

Stones are rearranged within the territories so that the vacant points lie in easily countable units, usually fives or tens. It is normal for you to

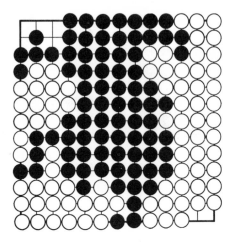

Diagram 37

count your opponent's territory and for him to count yours. Totals are then compared and one subtracted from the other to give the margin of victory.

The rearranging process has been done for the game above in Diagram 37. You can see how much easier it is to count now. Black has 5 points; White has 2. *Black wins by 3.*

One final thing. When the stones are cleared away each player should remove his own stones. This is not a convention but it does avoid bumping of knuckles.

5 Basic tactics

CAPTURING

There are two common capturing mistakes that beginners have to watch. One is trying all the time to capture, with atari—atari—atari. The other is failing to recognize when stones are dead and cannot avoid capture.

   You should also beware of capturing just for the sake of it. The Go literature is peppered with proverbs like 'Win the group, lose the game'. But assuming that a capture is worthwhile, or if you really can't resist the temptation, you should give some priority to learning the seven basic methods of capture.

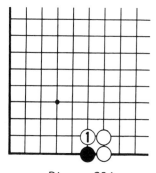

Diagram 38A

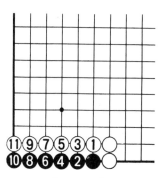

Diagram 38B

1. Atari using the edge of the board

Never forget the special feature of the edge of the board, which can be your friend, but can also be your worst enemy. You will meet it in some of the other methods of capturing as well.

   In Diagram 38A White has just played atari at 1. The black stone in atari is effectively captured, and Black should not throw away more stones trying to save it. Diagram 38B shows why. You can see how the edge of the board plays its part.

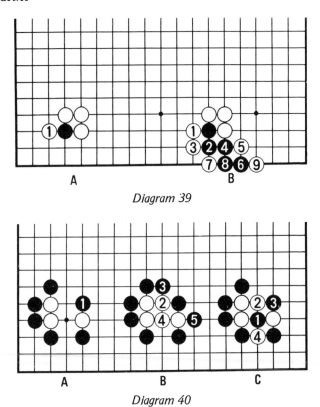

Diagram 39

Diagram 40

Diagrams 39A and 39B show a more complicated example of the same thing. Just imagine the position in 39A the other way round, with the black stone in atari facing the centre of the board. It could easily escape then.

2. Block (or geta)
Sometimes straightforward atari fails.

In Diagram 40A Black has to play 1 at just the right point in the enemy's escape path. This is the only move with which Black can capture White. White's efforts to escape get nowhere (B). This is called a *block* or, in Japanese, *geta*. The important thing to note is that playing the simple atari first fails: in Diagram C White is safe.

Geta is particularly common facing the centre of the board. Often it is the only means of capturing in this situation. In a sense what you are doing is placing a stone so that it has the same effect as the edge of the board would have.

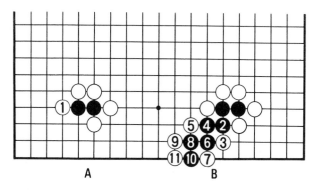

Diagram 41 Ladder

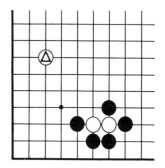

Diagram 42 Ladder breaker

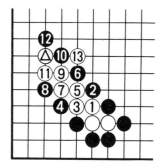

Diagram 43

3. Ladder (or shicho)

The atari of White 1 in Diagram 41A captures two black stones by chasing them (again) towards the edge. The name *ladder* comes from the resulting shape (41B). Although it is obviously bad to throw away more stones like this trying for a rescue, there is sometimes a way to bring it about.

In Diagram 42 the white stone already played at ⊿ lies in the path of a ladder, and is therefore known as a ladder breaker. You can see its effect in the next diagram. This stone provides the extra liberties White needs for survival, and now Black's position is in tatters, with cutting points all over the place e.g. at 13.

If it is Black to move in Diagram 42 he should capture the stones at once. He can also consider putting another ladder breaker, a stone of his own colour, in the path of the ladder, but White can do the same, and the position becomes very complicated. Of course when Black captures the two stones in Diagram 42 he is giving White a free move (⊿) on the side. This, in fact, is the main tactical significance of ladders.

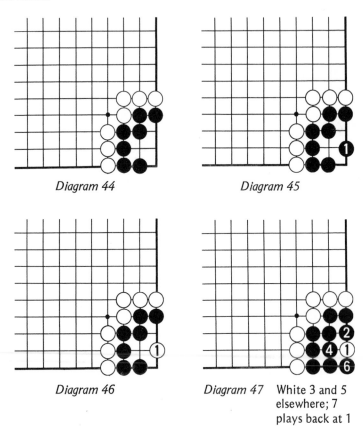

Diagram 44   Diagram 45

Diagram 46   Diagram 47   White 3 and 5
                                                elsewhere; 7
                                                plays back at 1

4. Oki

This is a method of capturing a whole group, once you have reduced it to one eye, as in Diagram 44. If it were Black's move he would rush to play 1 in Diagram 45. This gives him two eyes and life (and three points of territory).

However, if White has the first move then he plays at 1 and kills all the black stones (Diagram 46). For Black to capture the white stone (Diagram 47) would be a waste of time, because if White wants he can play back at 1 and remove all the black stones. Note that White wouldn't in fact do so, unless forced (e.g. to save part of his surrounding wall from capture). He, and Black, should just treat the black group as dead stones.

Some further information on how to play oki to kill will be given later in this chapter under 'Making Two Eyes'. Incidentally there is no standard English term for *oki* but it means something like 'placement'.

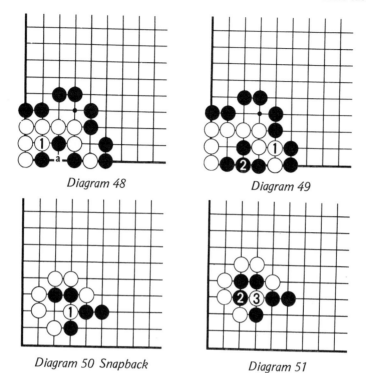

Diagram 48

Diagram 49

Diagram 50 Snapback

Diagram 51

5. Damezumari (or shortage of liberties)

In Diagram 48 Black is not allowed to play at *a* after White 1, because his stones would then have no liberties, i.e. this would be suicide. This gives White time to get two eyes. When White's group is attacked from the outside White can capture at *a*, and this gives him two eyes. If White plays the wrong move — at 1 in Diagram 49 — Black can play 2. This leads to the same oki shape as Diagram 46; so White will die.

6. Snapback (or uttegaeshi)

In Diagram 50 White 1 is a throw-in (horikomi) which captures the two black stones. Of course Black can capture the white stone, but White plays straight back (Diagram 51) and removes *three* black stones. Snapback is rather an appropriate name. Incidentally if the position in Diagram 50 remains till the end of the game the two black stones are simply removed as dead: White does not have to fill in their last liberty, which is logical if you consider Diagram 51. Meanwhile Black should not play the position out, thinking it makes no difference. He should keep 2 in Diagram 51 as a ko threat, threatening to save his stones by connecting at 3.

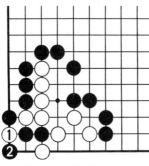
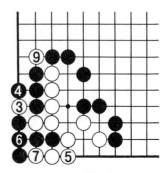

Diagram 52 Oi otoshi   Diagram 53   8 at 3

7. Oi otoshi (or robber's attack)

This refers to a horikomi situation taken one stage further.

In Diagram 52 White 1 is a sacrifice stone (*sute ishi*) which Black must take: Diagram 53. Now White cannot capture straight back, as in the snapback, because the black stones have two liberties. Instead he plays at 3, forcing Black to capture again (the purpose of sacrificing these stones is to make the opponent fill in his own liberties). Now White 5 is a *tesuji*—a move which exploits all the features of the shapes of the black and the white stones, and therefore the best move. (White 1 in Diagram 50 was also tesuji.) Black 6 is a mistake. After White 7 and Black 8, White 9 captures ten black stones. Notice that White would have failed if he had not sacrificed a stone at 3 first. If for instance he played 3 at 5, Black would then play at 3 and get an extra liberty — the cut at 9 no longer works.

Black should have played at 9 instead of 6; then after White 7 again and Black 8, White 6 captures only three stones. As you see, oi otoshi is rather complicated. It tends to look a bit like a conjuring trick at first, but it is very common; so you should try to understand it, especially the use of sacrifice stones.

CONNECTING

You often see players waving their hands over the board, ready to play a stone but not quite sure where to play. The odds are they are wondering how to connect.

A solid connection is safe but slow. You might be able to make more efficient use of your stones by making a loose connection. There are no absolute guidelines about when and how to do this. The best we can do is look at some possibilities, so that you will understand such moves when you see them.

Of course whether you should connect at all is a separate problem.

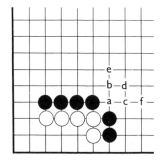

Diagram 54 Ways of connecting

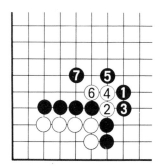

Diagram 55

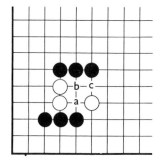

Diagram 56 Bamboo joint

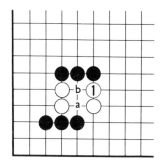

Diagram 57

Consider the weak point at *a* in Diagram 54 first of all. Black can play
at *a*, but he might also consider *b*, *c*, *d*, *e*, or *f*. They are all quite safe at
the moment. For example, if Black plays at *d* and White plays at *a* then
Black can play as in Diagram 55, and Black 7 (geta) captures the white
stones. Black could also have captured by shicho.

The advantage of the loose method of connecting is that the connecting stone has more influence on what goes on in the centre of the board.
Precisely how depends on the game. You will find examples of different
cases in this book and in your own games.

In Diagram 56 Black is threatening to cut White in two with *a*, White *b*,
Black *c*. White could defend against this by playing at *a*, but he usually
finds it more efficient to play at *c*, as in Diagram 57. This shape is known
as a *bamboo joint*. (Don't worry about remembering all these terms, by
the way.) If Black *a*, White *b*, or vice versa.

Finally you can connect by capturing, as in Diagram 58. Black 1 is a
geta, and when the top white stone is captured the black group will be
united. Imagine the situation if White had been able to play at 1. Then

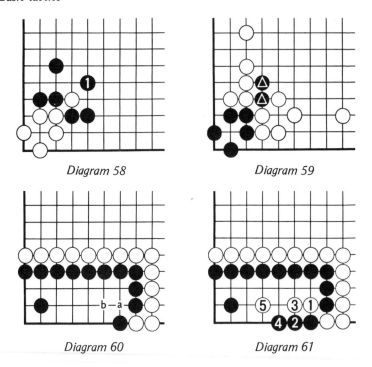

Diagram 58   Diagram 59

Diagram 60   Diagram 61

Black would be split into two, and would have to make two eyes for both his groups at once, always an unpleasant task.

To understand the primary reason for connecting and capturing, therefore, contrast this position with the one in Diagram 59.

Here White's groups on either side of the cutting stones ◮ are already secure (two-eye shape). He has no immediate need to connect, and thus no need to capture. He should not do so until there is no bigger play on the board. Capturing would get him a mere 4 or 5 points; so this would be an endgame play. The essential thing is that capturing here has no strategic value.

SEALING OFF TERRITORY

The moves that seal off territory on the edge of the board require special care, simply because of the edge.

First of all the case when you *must* connect.

In Diagram 60 a connecting move to protect the cutting point at *a* is essential. (Remember that the solid connection at *a* may not be the best; connection at *b* for instance gives better eye shape, though at the cost of two ko threats.) But why essential?

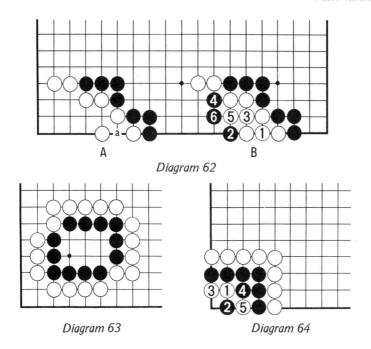

Diagram 62

Diagram 63   *Diagram 64*

Otherwise White can play the sequence up to 5 in Diagram 61; this geta ensures the capture of the black stones and ruin of Black's territory. If Black already has a stone in this area, say at 2, 4, or 5, he does not need to connect, because then White's invasion fails.

Now the case when you must *not* connect:

Diagram 62. For White to play at *a* in A would be to invite disaster by the sequence in B. He should first play at 3, allowing Black to take at 1. This is then a ko fight over one stone.

Every game has several positions like these. Sometimes there is a complicated sequence involving horikomi or oi otoshi, but basically they are all variations on the themes above. Usually all you need is a slight pause before playing to make sure you are not falling into a trap. If error does creep in it's up to you to make sure it doesn't happen again.

MAKING TWO EYES

Provided that it is not in the corner, and provided that there are no false eyes or other defects in your formation, *you can usually form two eyes in an area if it has at least six points of territory.* Try it in Diagram 63. The corner is different, as you can see in Diagram 64, where White 5 captures the black wall.

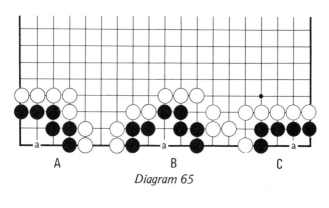

A   B   C

Diagram 65

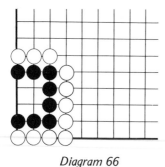

Diagram 66

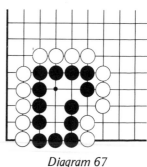

Diagram 67

With less than six points the shape of the area, or who has first move, becomes important. Five or four points in a straight line is completely safe, even in the corner, but with an area of three points first move is crucial.

The fates of five points in the shape of Diagram 65A, four points in the shape of Diagram 65B, or three points in any shape (a straight line in Diagram 65C), all depend on who has first move. The vital point in each case is *a*. A black stone here secures two eyes; a white stone kills the black group.

Four points in a square are always dead (Diagram 66). The best Black can do is to form a three-point shape, but then his opponent has first move.

Bent-four shapes like that in Diagram 67 however, are always alive, with one exception — in the corner. This will be explained in a moment.

First of all, why should first move be so important?

The white group in Diagram 68 is dead, because when White captures at *a* the shape left by the captured black stones is one of the five-point shapes where first move decides life or death. And of course Black now has first move: see Diagram 69.

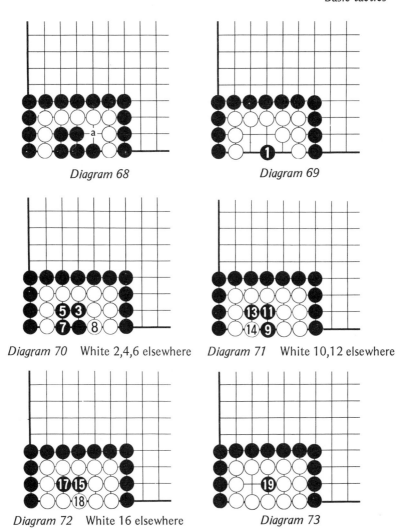

Diagram 68

Diagram 69

Diagram 70 White 2,4,6 elsewhere

Diagram 71 White 10,12 elsewhere

Diagram 72 White 16 elsewhere

Diagram 73

Let us imagine Black has to capture this group completely. (Assume for instance his outside wall is threatened with capture.) He therefore plays in this group at 3, 5, and 7 atari (Diagram 70). White must capture again.

Black plays back with 9, 11, 13 atari. After White takes (Diagram 71) Black 15 goes straight back. 17 is atari, White takes (Diagram 72); and by now you can see how Black can play at 19 in Diagram 73 and capture White next move. If in these sequences White plays even more moves inside his group he just precipitates the end.

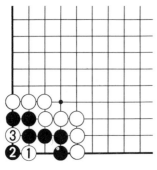

Diagram 74

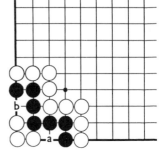

Diagram 75

Bent four in the corner

Along with seki this is one of the exceptions in Go that you should take the trouble to learn. Like seki the situation itself is straightforward; it is the ruling in the final position that has to be remembered.

In Diagram 74 White has played at 1, the weak point of this formation and after Black 2, White 3 produces a ko which affects the life of the black group.

There is no problem about this. Compare however the position in Diagram 75. Here if Black plays at *a* (or *b*) then White *b* (or *a*) wins the black group. If White plays first at *a* or *b* his four stones are captured, of course, but that leaves the bent-four shape, and White can play back to force a ko as in Diagram 74.

The point is, this is a ko that only White can start. He can therefore wait until the end of the game, when supposedly all ko threats have been eliminated, before playing the ko, and can thus ensure winning the ko and the group.

This is not an entirely satisfactory assumption, but the ruling is that in positions like those in Diagram 75, *where one player can wait till the end of the game* before starting the ko, the group at a disadvantage (the black group here) is unconditionally dead. So in Diagram 75 at the end of the game the black stones are just removed without fighting the ko. This is rather complicated, but like seki it is fairly common; so it is worth learning.

REVIEW PROBLEMS

The following problems (answers on page 43) cover many of the points discussed so far. Some of them are a little tricky, but they are all situations that crop up frequently in games. You should try first of all to work them out in out in your head (this is called 'reading' in Go), but don't worry how many

you score. The important thing is that you should understand the answers.
If you do get them all right though you must have jumped to at least 20-kyu!

When you have done these problems don't rush on to the next chapter.
First play a few games — against yourself if you have no opponent. This
should help you to absorb everything you have learnt so far, which is really
quite a lot, and to store up some experience. Even if you start on a smaller
board you should try to get in at least a couple of games on the full 19x19
board, because the rest of the book is based on this. After all, you've got
to start playing some time!

Probably you will still find difficulty in deciding when the game is over.
Experience is the only way round this. The rules are a bit vague on this
point; so don't feel that it is your fault.

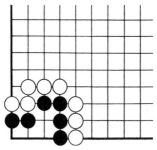

Diagram 76

(a) Does Black need another move
for life, or can he afford to play
elsewhere?

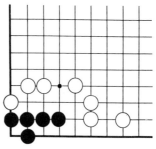

Diagram 77

(b) White to play and kill Black
(i.e. stop him getting two eyes).

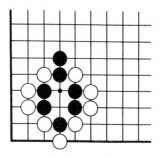

Diagram 78

(c) White to play. What is his best
move?

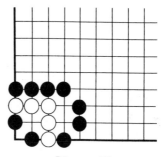

Diagram 79

(d) Can White live here?

Basic tactics

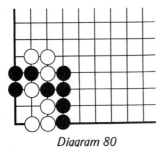

Diagram 80

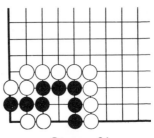

Diagram 81

(e) What is the best White can do in this situation?

(f) Does Black need another move in the corner to ensure life? Can he gain more territory here?

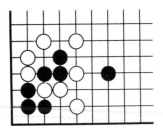

Diagram 82

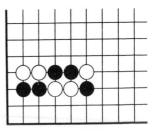

Diagram 83

(g) How can the black stones escape to the centre?

(h) How can White capture the two black stones at the top?

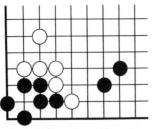

Diagram 84

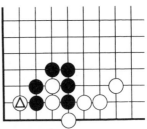

Diagram 85

(i) How can Black connect his corner stones to those on the side?

(j) To stop Black getting all the corner White wants to join his main group to ⊘. How can he do it?

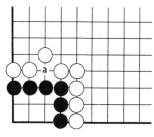

Diagram 86

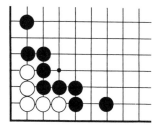

Diagram 87

(k) What is White's best play in the corner? Note the liberty at *a*.

(l) White to play and live? This is not so easy as it looks.

ANSWERS

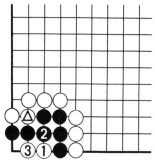

Diagram 88

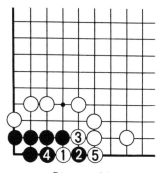

Diagram 89

(a) Yes, Black needs another move here. If he had a stone at ⊛ he would be all right, but here White 1 is atari, which gives White time to play at 3.

(b) The sequence of 1 and 3 makes a false eye for Black, even though he can capture stone 1. Black 2 at 3 fails also, when White connects at 2.

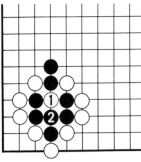

Diagram 90

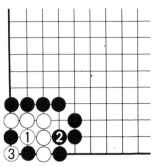

Diagram 91

(c) White 1 is best, as this captures most of the black stones. If Black 2, White plays 3 at 1 (a snapback). White 1 at 2 captures only one stone, as Black can then connect at 1.

(d) White 1 works because now Black is not allowed to play at 3 (suicide). After Black 2 atari, White captures at 3 to make two eyes. If it had been Black to play first, he would kill White by playing move 1 at 3.

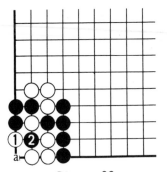

Diagram 92

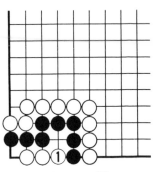

Diagram 93

(e) White can make a ko with 1. If Black loses the ko (i.e. if he cannot play at 2 then *a*) White captures the three stones on the edge, and thus saves his corner stones. White 1 at 2 loses to Black 1 atari.

(f) No; Black is alive already. After White 1 it is seki; so by the rules both Black and White are alive. However, if Black played at 1 he would have 6 points. Now he has none.

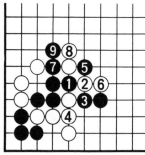

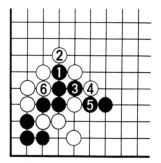

Diagram 94A RIGHT   Diagram 94B WRONG

(g) The order of moves is important. Black 1 in Diagram 94A is correct. Black 1 in 94B is wrong because it fills in a black liberty, so that now White 4 is atari, and White can defend against Black 5 by capturing.

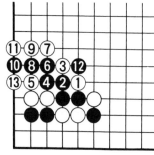

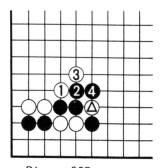

Diagram 95A RIGHT   Diagram 95B WRONG

(h) White can capture with a ladder. If Black resists he runs into the edge of the board. White 1 in Diagram 95B is wrong, because after Black 4 the stone ⊘ is in atari. White has to defend this, which gives Black time to escape.

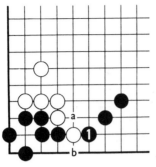

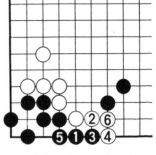

Diagram 96A RIGHT   *Diagram 96B* WRONG

(i) Black 1 in Diagram 96A is the only way to connect. It leaves the alternative points *a* and *b*. If White plays *b*, Black *a* captures the two white stones on the edge. Therefore White should now play *a* and let Black connect at *b*. Direct methods such as 1 in Diagram 96B very often fail in Go.

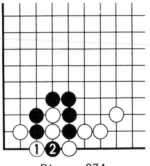

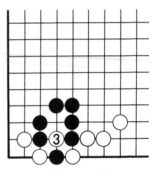

Diagram 97A   *Diagram 97B*

(j) White 1 works even though it lets Black capture two stones at 2. The reason is that White can capture straight back at 3. (This of course is not ko.) White 1 at 2 saves the two white stones, but after Black 1 the much bigger corner is lost.

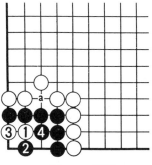

Diagram 98A

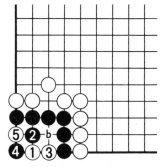

Diagram 98B

(k) This is similar to the position mentioned on page 37. The difference is in the liberty at *a*. White fails now if he plays at 1 in Diagram 98A, because with the extra liberty Black can play at 4. White should therefore play as in 98B, which is ko. Note that if the black group had *two* or more liberties on the outside it is not even ko because he could now play at *b*. Compare (d).

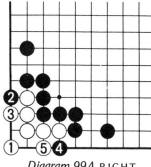

Diagram 99A RIGHT

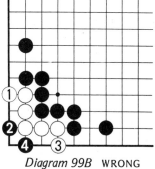

Diagram 99B WRONG

(l) White 1 in Diagram 99A guarantees two eyes. It follows the proverb: 'Play in the centre of a symmetrical formation'. White 1 in 99B makes more space for the white group, but the shape resulting after Black 2 and 4 is bent four in the corner.

6 How to start a game

A game normally begins with stones being placed at strategic points to map out prospective territories. This stage is called the *fuseki*, and it takes somewhere between 6 and 50 moves.

The fuseki covers the whole board, and because of the immense variety that this brings there are really no standard fusekis to remember. You can really do your own thing.

The corners are different. They are strategically the best areas on the board, and both players tend to contest them. Over the centuries very many standard sets of corner plays have evolved. These are called *joseki* (fixed stones), and the need to distinguish between fuseki and joseki is why we tend not to speak of the 'opening' of a game.

You do not have to learn thousands of josekis. You could easily become a top-notch player with knowledge of less than, say, 50 josekis. For the moment you need not learn any: it is more important to understand the strategic principles behind them. Even if you do know a few thousand your efforts are wasted if you can't apply them properly within the overall context of fuseki.

Anyway there are four corners on the board. If you don't know the right joseki in one corner you can always play elsewhere. On top of that josekis are very much subject to the whims of fashion, even among the professionals.

FUSEKI

There are two basic principles underlying the fuseki. These you must learn.
  1. *Corner, Side, then Centre.*
  2. *Start on the third and fourth lines.*

These principles have been challenged, notably in the 1930s by the professionals Go Sei Gen and Minoru Kitani, who horrified the old masters with their new fuseki (shin-fuseki). You will hear a lot of this, probably because the Japanese don't seem to have recovered from the shock of the elders being doubted. These revolutionaries were really reacting against the overstrict application of the ancient principles. The modern style, a blend of mostly old and a little new, allows a fair degree of flexibility.

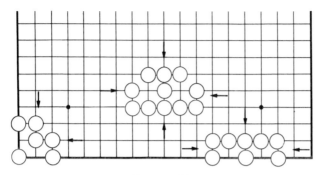

Diagram 100

Corner, Side, Centre

Both in even games (no handicap stones) and in handicap games you should occupy the corners before the sides, and the sides before the centre. Why?

As you can see in Diagram 100 fewer stones are required to form two eyes, the nucleus of a safe territory, in the corner than on the side. In other words, it is easier. Similarly fewer stones are required on the side than in the centre. In addition the centre is open to attack on four sides, the sides on three, and the corner on only two.

Since it is advantageous to keep your stones linked, however tenuously, you should extend from the corners you occupy to the side, rather than just play anywhere on the side. And then you should advance towards the centre by extending from your side positions.

This orderly progression may be interrupted by a joseki, where tactical considerations overrule strategy, but when the joseki is over you must still go back to the corners, sides, then centre.

One of the revolutionary concepts of the shin-fuseki was to play the first move on the centre point (*tengen*). This is still done occasionally, but Go Sei Gen abandoned it with the comment that it was basically a sound move, but too difficult to exploit properly. So he went back to playing in the corners first.

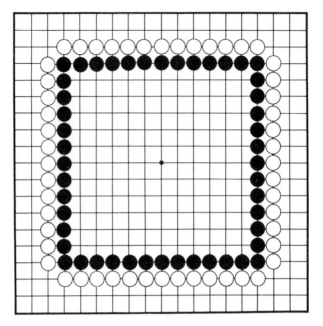

Diagram 101

Third and fourth Lines

In Diagram 101 White has surrounded the two outside lines by putting his stones on the third line from the edge. Black has surrounded the centre by playing on the fourth line. The centre area may look bigger, but in fact White has 140 points to Black's 121. Since White has had to use four more stones we can regard this as an equal distribution of territory.

This balance is lost, however, if one player occupies the fifth line and the other the fourth, or the third and second respectively. Both players, therefore, generally prefer to start on the third and fourth lines, so as to achieve a balance — whatever the opponent may be doing.

For the reasons already mentioned play will start in the corners, and then go to the sides; but you should appreciate that *a stone on the fourth line is looking towards the centre*, while *a stone on the third line is oriented towards territory on the edge.*

You should also realize that it is bad to allow your opponent to seal off side territory on the fourth line, and that at the beginning it is a waste of time to make territory on the second line.

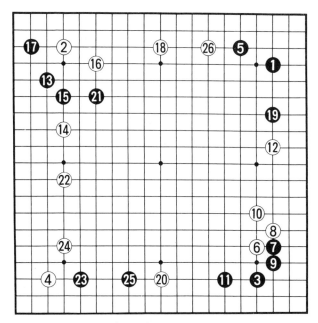

Diagram 102 R.J. Smith (Black) v. P.T. Manning. Marlborough 1974

It is better to stake out territories loosely than to form impenetrable walls around one corner. For instance to seal off 30 points in the corner takes 14 stones. With 14 moves your opponent can virtually secure the rest of the board.

The benefit of playing first in an area is enormous. In fuseki two or three moves are sufficient to make a territory secure. You can see this if you consider the game above.

This is a game between two strong amateurs. Not all of the moves are the best possible, but they are still in line with the two basic principles. Moves 3 plus 6-12 in the bottom right and 2 plus 13-18 are two popular josekis. The bottom left corner is also a kind of joseki.

Move 21 is the only one which really goes against the basics, and in fact it is not a good move so early. It would be better in the region of 22 to prevent White from making a formidable *moyo* (territorial framework) on the left side.

White 20 is also suspect, for it gives Black room to squeeze in with 23 and 25, but in general this is all sound play.

How to start a game

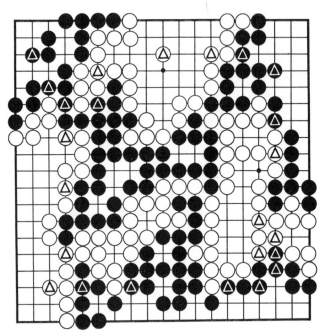

Diagram 103

This is the same game when finished. The stones marked with a triangle are the stones played in the fuseki in Diagram 102. White 2 and 20 are missing because they were captured.

You can see how the fuseki stones have determined the basic shape of the territories, and how, therefore, these few stones were sufficient to secure these areas.

Notice also how White's stones 6 and 10 on the right, being centre oriented, have led to territory in the centre rather than on the side.

White has made territory on the fourth line on the left side, the result of the poor black move 21. However White's weak move 20 was enveloped on the bottom side, an area dominated early on by Black. White had no room to make a base for this stone to get two eyes, and its other means of escape, running away to the centre, was hampered by its being on the third instead of the fourth line.

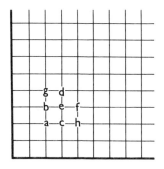

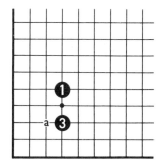

Diagram 104   *Diagram 105*

Incidentally White won by 5 points, counting captured stones.

Things do not always go as smoothly as this, of course. Professionals in particular are fond of swapping territories (this is called *furikawari*) but the above game is typical of sound amateur play.

JOSEKI

There is room here for only a few pointers about josekis (corner plays) but it should be possible to set you off on the right path.

The first move is usually at one of the points marked in Diagram 104. They all have special names (if you want to learn them *a* is *san-san, e* is *hoshi, b* and *c* are *komoku, d* and *f takamoku,* and *g* and *h mokuhazushi*). Moves *a* and *e* are complete corner moves in themselves. *a* takes all the corner territory; *e* takes all the corner influence—i.e. builds up a wall that will have a big influence on the centre. But that's all these moves do. Each of moves *b, d,* or *g* (the other points are equivalent) requires one more move to control the corner, but if that move is made it gives control of both the territory and the influence in the corner. These moves also look towards extensions on the side.

A two-stone corner enclosure (or *shimari*) is very powerful, and the opponent usually stops it by playing on the point needed to make it. His move is then called a *kakari* (hanging, i.e. onto the corner stone). Diagram 105 shows how Black makes a shimari from takamoku. White should play at 3, or sometimes *a*, if he wants to contest the corner.

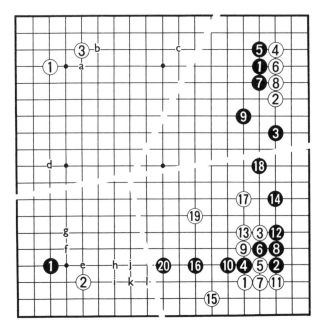

Diagram 106

In the top left of Diagram 106 you see the usual shimari from komoku. It could also be at *a* or *b*. White is now aiming to extend to *c* or *d*.

In the top right you can see how it is possible to build a strong wall facing the centre using hoshi as a basis, although this surrenders the corner territory.

In the bottom left White has played a kakari against Black's komoku. This and *e* are the usual ways of attacking the corner stone. In the old days Black commonly played his next move around *f* or *g*, but nowadays it is more usual to 'pincer' the white stone by playing at *h*, *i*, *j*, *k*, or *l*.

In the bottom right is a common joseki developing from mokuhazushi. This is one of the very few complete josekis to have a name, by the way — it is called *taisha*, and it has the reputation of being the most difficult of all.

You can pick up other josekis from games, or get books on them, but you should remember that they don't really come alive except in the context of the whole board, as we shall see in the next chapter.

7 The middle game

There are so many strategic and tactical considerations in the middle game that it is impossible even to mention them all. What we shall do, however, is to look at some concepts which will be of particular help in appreciating games by stronger players. Studying such games is one of the quickest ways to improve.

We shall consider these concepts within the framework of an amateur game from the 19th European Championship held in 1975 in Austria. This was between (Black) Jim Bates, 3-dan from London and (White) Michael Kitsos, 4-dan from Greece.

The time limit in this game was 3 hours each, plus 60 seconds *byoyomi*. (Professionals usually have 6 or 10 hours each.) Each player can spend any amount of time he likes on any move (chess clocks are used) but when his 3 hours are used up he switches over to byoyomi (= second-counting, pronounced with the by- sounding like the initial sound in 'beauty'). This means that he is allowed a maximum of 60 seconds for each move. A time-keeper counts off the seconds. Players usually arrange it so that the last 50 or so endgame plays come in byoyomi.

The basic theme of this game is that Black gained a big advantage in fuseki, mainly because of White's incorrect play. Black concentrated on the third line; White emphasized the centre. However, with the last move of the fuseki Black made a slight error which gave White the chance to cut off a group and subject it to attack. Fortunately for Black the advantage he had gained in fuseki was just sufficient to offset the losses he incurred in weathering the attack.

His concentration on the third line left Black weak in the centre. He had to play there eventually, but when he did it was this stone which was cut off. Black's lack of balance of stones on the third and fourth lines thus told against him, but he had calculated that if he had only one weak group he would have time to look after it and to attend to other matters at the same time.

White's view is that he does not expect to kill Black's weak group. He is content if, by chasing it, he can make territory in such a way that Black is too busy looking after his weak group to reduce White's territory. Because White's fuseki emphasized the centre it is of course White who calls the tune in any fighting there.

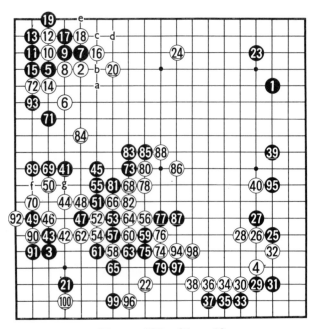

Diagram 107   67 on 58

Diagram 107 (1—100)
The sequence in the top left corner up to White 20 is joseki, Black taking
the corner in return for White's outside influence. The exchange of Black
a for White *b* is often played now, but is optional. Later in this game
Black regrets not having played it.

Black's corner territory looks small in contrast to White's imposing wall,
but there is a very important consideration here which will apply throughout this and every game. This is the concept of *sente* (sen-tay).

You are said to have sente in a position when your move is so threatening that the opponent must answer it and play the last move in that position.
If you have to play last in a situation you are said to be in *gote* (go-tay).

The advantage of having sente is that after playing in one area you can
play first in another part of the board. Players are usually willing to sacrifice a few points just to keep sente, as Black has done in this joseki. White
played first here (move 2) but also has to play last (20).

The kind of thinking involved with sente and gote is this. If Black
captures stone 18 by playing *c*, White plays *d*, Black *e*, and now since
White has no weak points to patch up he can play elsewhere. He thus has
sente and Black has gained a measly two points.

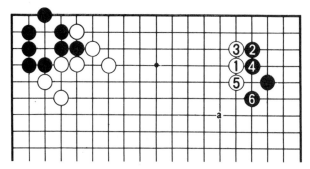

Diagram 108

Black, however, keeps sente and makes a shimari at 21 (bottom left).
White 22 and 24 are questionable. They allow Black to get two shimaris,
something which is considered to be a big advantage.

White 24 is too small in scale. In other words, because of his strength
in the top left corner White could afford to be more ambitious in staking
out territory on the upper side. One way of playing would be to use the
joseki of Diagram 108 above for move 22. Here Black has basically the same
corner shape, but White's wall of three stones is threatening to take a much
bigger area at the top, and now White can play 22 if he wants.

Note: if White had no stones in the top left he should play at 24 to
finish this joseki in gote. The point *a* is the other vital point in this area for
both players.

White was flummoxed by Black 29, as he didn't know how the joseki
goes from now on. What follows therefore is his own invention. It is not
altogether bad for him, but Black has sente. Incidentally Black thought for
a very long time over 37. He was reluctant to give White the extra strength
of 38 but decided his frail corner group needed a bit more space.

Black 39: (centre right): The normal extension from the shimari in the
top right is to 95 but Black properly follows the proverb which says *keep
away from enemy thickness*, i.e. White's strong wall at the bottom.

Black 41 (centre left) was the crunch move. Having followed the proverb
with 39 Black ignores it with this move and gets into difficulties. This is the
end of the fuseki—the middle-game fighting now begins. Let us survey the
position so far.

His last move apart none of Black's play can be criticized. He has all four
corners (there is another proverb which goes: *If you lose all four corners,
resign!*). His overall position though is a bit low, being concentrated on the
3rd line, and so it is correct to play move 41 on the 4th line to achieve
some balance and have a say in the centre.

The middle game

As for White he dominates the centre, and has already done enough to make sure that Black will not get all the side territory, but move 24 was too small, and he faltered in the bottom right corner. Black is therefore ahead, simply because he has made fewer mistakes.

Some explanation is needed as to why White has a poor position in the bottom corner. After all it looks very much like the situation in the top left. The difference is in the two black stones 25 and 27, which provide lots of possibilities. They are said to have *aji* (= taste), good aji for Black, bad for White. As long as the situation remains unsettled here White will feel uneasy about it.

You should try to leave as much aji as possible if it is favourable to you. Think twice, therefore, before playing positions out. As the game develops you may (in fact usually) regret playing one way because you can see how much better it would have been to play another way. Keep your options open. This is why Black just leaves his two stones on the right for the time being, and incidentally why White doesn't attack the Black group in the bottom right corner just yet.

But back to the left side. There is a defect in the relationship of Black 41 to the lower shimari: it can be cut off. White spots this. White 42 and 44 isolate Black 41, and now it has to make two eyes on its own. In doing this Black will naturally try to counterattack the White group developing from 42 and 44.

White 50 was therefore a rude shock to Black. It takes the base on the edge away from Black's two-stone group and it also makes good eye shape for the white group, especially in conjunction with White 70.

White cut Black in two with 66, even though this separated his own groups too. The point is, the white groups are much stronger. See the effect of White 50.

Note that Black did not connect at 67 just to save his stones from being captured (it is only worth 1 point to do this) but because if White captured them his groups would be reunited. After White 68 Black's weak group is looking very unhealthy.

With the series of moves around 74 White hopes to settle the aji here before continuing to attack the group above. Black, however, tries to keep the aji, hence stones 77 and 87. Note after White 84 how the exchange of *a* and *b* in Diagram 107 would have helped Black now: Black *a* would aim at a cutting point between 6 and 84. White would probably answer differently if it were played now.

White 90 is necessary to make two eyes; otherwise after Black 90 one is false: e.g. White at *f* Black at *g* or vice versa.

Black 93 (upper left): White could play to the left of 72 to stop Black connecting and saving his group, but Black's group is a bit healthier now

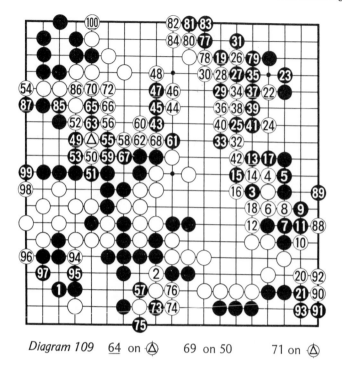

Diagram 109 <u>64</u> on ⊛   69 on 50   71 on ⊛

and Black might ignore it and play at 94, devastating White's only large territory. In other words, White wants to keep sente.

White 96 is sneaky (it looks small but has some nasty threats against the corner), but White 100 was expected. It is a common advanced tactic called yosu-miru (look-and-see) played to see how your opponent will answer before you decide how to continue.

After 98 White has built up a large and almost secure territory on the right (but watch the aji of 25 and 27) simply because he has been able to push against Black's weak group all the time.

Diagram 109 (101—200)
Note that the moves in this diagram are numbered 1 to 100. This is normal practice, and makes them easier to read.

See now how Black uses the aji of his original 25 and 27 (next to 7 in Diagram 109). He launches a small attack on the white stones on the right-hand side of White's large territory. He plays 13 and 17 to start sealing off the territory in the top right, and with sente too, so that he is able to take the last big point (19) left over from the fuseki before it was so rudely inter-rupted by the middle game. Black only has to keep his head to win now.

In fact both players will have been counting the game throughout. This is a great help in deciding how to play next. For instance if you are behind, take risks. Of course the counting cannot be accurate, but the better the players the more accurate it will be. Let us count the position after Black 19 in this diagram.

The large Black territory on the right is worth about 35 points. The two black groups in the bottom right and top left corners are worth about 8 points each. The bottom left corner group is worth 15 points (but if Black can play here first it will be worth about 8 points more). The weak group in the centre should be good for 5 points. That gives Black a total of 35 + 8 + 8 + 15 + 5 = 71. Add to this 3 prisoners; grand total = 74.

White's large territory on the right is worth 35 points, the little one on the left 5 points, and he has 2 captured pieces. Total so far 42. That means he has to get about 30 points from the territory at the top. At the moment it is looking good for only 15, but of course all these figures can change as the game progresses.

White 22 and 24 are similar to his previous tactic in the opposite corner. Black is much stronger here, however, and can easily connect on the edge if need be. He therefore attacks the white stones; but he has to be very careful not to let the fight spill over to the centre, where it may affect his still-weak group. For his part White wants either to reduce Black's side territory or to increase the size of his own territory at the top. For the latter course, how-ever, he must keep sente.

With 37 Black is sacrificing a little to be certain of getting sente for move 43, a dual-purpose move that reduces White's territory and helps the weak group. If White had had sente to play here he would have got the necessary 30 points.

Black 47 is bad. It eliminates aji for no good reason. If Black had avoided this move, and play had developed appropriately to the left of this wall of three stones, Black might have been able to jump to 48.

Black 49. Simple connection at 54 (top left) looks safer, but Black is still striving to make the best move possible, despite the risks.

Black 57: too greedy. The weak group needs at least one more move. To make matters worse 61 was a downright blunder, because after 62 Black still has to make two eyes for his group, and doesn't have time to make the connection at 68.

White 64 is the horikomi tesuji, the purpose of which is to make a false eye. (A black stone at Ⓐ would make a good eye.) This is very common and useful; so you should memorize it.

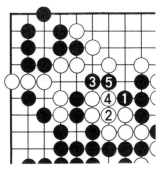

Diagram 110

White 70 is absolutely necessary to save his territory, otherwise Black could save his dead stones; see Diagram 110.

After the loss of his four stones and the consequent enlargement of White's territory, Black is only just ahead. He is lucky to come out of his blunder with sente.

The fighting has died down now. All groups are secure and the endgame stage is starting. This is called *yose* (yo-say), and is the time when players seal off their own territories and nibble away at their opponent's.

This stage has its own special tactics. What both players do now is to play first in those areas where they can secure the most points but trying to keep sente as long as possible. For instance Black 73 is big and is sente. This allows Black to play first in another large area (top centre).

Black 87 hands over sente at last to White, but this is a very big move; so it is worth it. You have to surrender sente sometime. White now plays all his sente moves and then plays 100 in gote.

Diagram 111 (201—245)
The game is really finished after Black 217, but White is behind; so he tries a ko fight at 18 in an effort to catch up a point or two. He is wasting his time, but it must be remembered that both players are in byoyomi (60 seconds a move); accurate play is not always possible.

Apart from taking and retaking the ko all the other plays now are ko threats.

White 44 fills in a dame, signifying that he surrenders the ko (he has to fill this point in eventually after *a* and *b* are filled in; so it is counted as a kind of dame) and Black 45 fills in the ko.

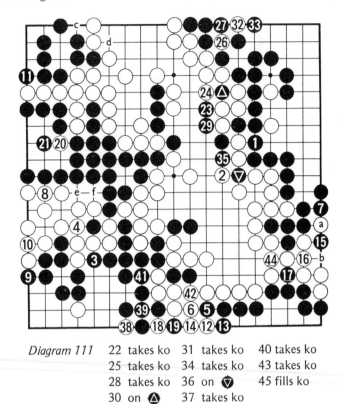

Diagram 111

22 takes ko	31 takes ko	40 takes ko
25 takes ko	34 takes ko	43 takes ko
28 takes ko	36 on ▼	45 fills ko
30 on ▲	37 takes ko	

The dame are now filled in. Black has to fill in at *a* after White *b*, and White *d* is necessary after Black *c*. The only other dame are at *e* and *f*. Dead stones are removed (12 black and 5 white) and counting begins. Black has 10 more points than White, but he had to give White 5½ points start to offset the advantage he had in playing first, so the final result is that Black wins by 4½ points.

You should replay this game sometime. If you can absorb the concepts of sente and aji you will improve enormously, but (fortunately) there are still many other things you can learn.

Now that you've seen how the game goes what do you say about Black 41? How about playing it one point lower down; or even at 119, aiming at invasion of the white area on the top edge? Think about it!

8 Unusual positions

We have already mentioned some of the exceptional positions in Go: ko, seki, bent four in the corner. These all occur frequently, ko especially so, but there are a few other positions that occur only rarely. These will be dealt with here.

Most of the special cases involve a ko, and since they can prove rather confusing it might be useful first to review the basic ko.

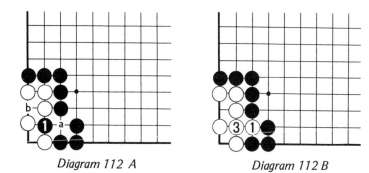

Diagram 112 A   Diagram 112 B

DIRECT KO

A ko fight is going on in Diagram 112A that concerns the life of the white group. Black has just captured at 1. White can make a ko threat 2, but Black can ignore it and win the ko by connecting at *a* (or by capturing at *b*) on move 3. White would then have two false eyes and therefore be dead. If, however, White can capture back at *a* he can secure life by ignoring Black's ko threat and then himself filling the ko at 3 in Diagram 112B.

The main feature of this type of ko, the commonest, is that either player can put an end to the ko immediately after capturing the ko stone by ignoring just one ko threat. The ko is then said to be direct for both players.

INDIRECT KO

It is possible, however, to have a ko fight in which only one player can win the ko immediately whereas the other player has to make at least one extra move before he is in a position to win the ko, which is a big disadvantage. The ko is then said to be indirect for the person who has to make the extra moves. An example is given in Diagram 113A.

Unusual positions

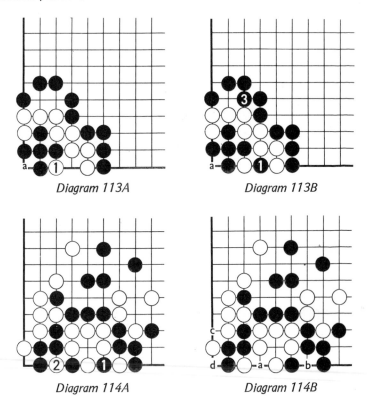

Diagram 113A   Diagram 113B

Diagram 114A   Diagram 114B

Here White can easily win the ko by ignoring just one black ko threat, i.e. by playing at *a*. Black, however, unfortunately has to take the ko, at 1 in Diagram 113B, ignore a white ko threat 2, then play 3 to put White in atari. This of course gives White the chance to take the ko back, and if Black is going to win this ko now he is going to have to ignore yet another ko threat. Black could not win the ko directly because if he. filled at *a* White would capture and have sufficient space to make two eyes. This type of ko is called a *yose-ko*, because it is usually left until the endgame (Yose is the endgame). Despite its awkwardness for Black there is nothing about such a ko that requires any special rulings

DOUBLE KO

Diagram 114A shows a *double* ko that develops from a popular joseki. Black can capture a stone at 1 and put White in atari. White cannot

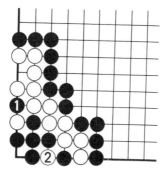

Diagram 115

capture straight back here because it is ko but he can immediately play at 2, in the other ko. The position now is shown in B.

White is now out of atari and of course Black cannot play straight back at *a*. He can play here if he makes a ko threat first but then White simply answers at *b* and we are back to the position of Diagram A. In other words Black can never capture White so long as White answers by taking back the other ko. White, however, can capture Black at any time he likes simply by filling in the outside liberty with *c* and *d*. The black stones are therefore dead (because they are ultimately capturable) and the white stones are alive, but this position is a marvellous source of ko threats for Black if there is a ko fight somewhere else on the board.

Compare now a different double ko: Diagram 115. Here capturing at 1 and 2 always leaves both sides with two liberties. Neither player can force the capture of the other's stones. It is stalemate, or seki. Like all sekis it is left just as it is at the end of the game. No dame are filled in, and no points are counted inside the seki (you are entitled to capture stones in a seki if this is possible, and count a point for each prisoner of course).

TRIPLE KO

This last type of seki/double ko could conceivably combined with another ko elsewhere on the board. If the result of the game then depends on who wins this third ko both players can use the double ko as an infinite source of ko threats so that the third ko, and hence the game, can never end. If he is far enough ahead one player can sacrifice one of the kos and so complete the game; otherwise it is declared no-contest.

Unusual positions

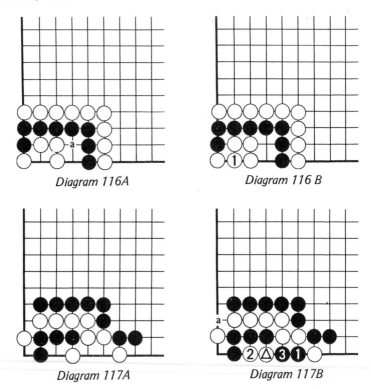

Diagram 116A

Diagram 116 B

Diagram 117A

Diagram 117B

10 000 YEAR KO

Yet another type of ko involving a possible seki is the 10 000 year ko (or *mannen ko*) shown in Diagram 116A. Here Black cannot try to capture White by playing first at *a*, since that would put himself in atari. He must first capture the ko to give himself an extra liberty, but this is a yose-ko of the type described above—not very good for Black. From White's point of view he can try to capture by playing at *a* but then Black takes the ko which is now *direct*. In other words White has done Black a favour. Since both players are reluctant to start the ko it is usually left for a long time, although 10 000 years seems a bit of an exaggeration. In fact what usually happens is that White plays 1 in Diagram 116B to produce a seki and put an end to the possibility of ko.

ETERNAL LIFE

This very interesting position is not a ko but it can have the same effect as triple ko, if it is Black to play. Of course if it is White to play he can

66

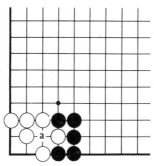

Diagram 118

live by playing *a* in Diagram 117B. (He can also live by playing 1, but only in seki). If Black has first move, he plays 1, then White, if he wants to keep his group alive, has to play at 2. If White simply captures Black 1, Black will play 2 and allow White to capture his five stones, because then Black can play back inside this 5-point space to kill White (see page 39). So White plays 2, and Black captures at 3, but then White can take Black's two stones by playing move 4 back at ⬠ and we are back where we started. Black can repeat the whole process as often as he likes by playing at 1, and so, unless either player is willing to make a sacrifice here, the game cannot end and it is declared no-contest. Any other similar cyclic situations are treated in the same way.

A KO WITH NO KO THREATS

If a position of the type in Diagram 118 occurred at the very end of the game and Black didn't have a single ko threat, White must nevertheless fill the ko at *a*, treating it as a dame.

There are some other positions that awkward people have devised to point up flaws in the rules. Theoretically they are right and if ever such positions arose in a game an *ad hoc* ruling would have to be made on the spot, but considering that such *ad hoc* rulings have been made ever since the first triple ko in 1582 without having to be applied to these freak positions, they can be regarded as too rare to bother about.

9 Handicaps

It is normal for the weaker player to take a handicap. This makes the game interesting for both players. In fact Go is one of the few games (golf is another) where the handicap system really compensates for different abilities, so that any two players can have a good game.

THE BASIC METHOD

Handicaps are calculated by giving one stone for every grade difference between the players. Thus a 6-kyu player gives 3 stones to a 9-kyu player (9—6) but he takes 7 stones from a 2-dan.

If there is one grade difference, i.e. one stone handicap, the weaker player simply plays first. If the handicap is two stones or more the stones must be put at specific points on the board, and this counts as Black's first move. The correct positions are shown on the next page.

The star points are used for up to 9 stones. The diagram opposite shows where they are placed. It is rare to play a game with more than 9 stones, because White can only win with a swindle after that. With 9 stones on the board there is still sufficient space for White to play strategically.

Experience shows that each handicap stone is worth about 10 points, so that if two ungraded players are playing and one wins consistently by say 50 points, he should try giving the other a 5-stone handicap.

Mathematicians are quick to latch on to the fact that the handicap scale is not really linear. For instance, with a 9-stone handicap the stones help each other, so that instead of being worth only 90 points they are really worth about 130 points. However the system works well in practice.

Since playing first is in itself equivalent to receiving a one-stone handicap, players of *equal* grading use a completely different kind of handicap to offset this advantage. This is known as *komi*, or *komidashi*.

KOMI

Nobody really knows how much the advantage of first move is worth, but it is considered to be about 5 points. In an even game, therefore, Black should give White 5 points start to make things equal. This start is the komi.

The usual method of giving this komi is for Black to place 5 of his stones in White's lid before the game begins. These then count as captured pieces for White, and in this way both players will remember to count the komi.

Sometimes komi is altered to 5½ or 4½ points to avoid the possibility of a drawn game (*jigo*). Professional tournaments have been played at each

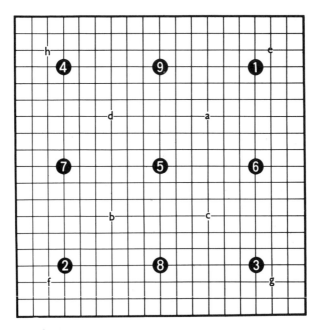

Diagram 119   Location of handicap stones

Handicap	Black stones must be placed at:
2 stones	1 and 2
3 stones	1, 2, and 3
4 stones	1, 2, 3, and 4
5 stones	1, 2, 3, 4, and 5
6 stones	1, 2, 3, 4, 6, and 7
7 stones	1, 2, 3, 4, 5, 6, and 7
8 stones	1, 2, 3, 4, 6, 7, 8, and 9
9 stones	1, 2, 3, 4, 5, 6, 7, 8, and 9
10-13 stones	The above 9 with each extra stone added in the order *a, b, c, d*
14-17 stones	The above 13 with each extra stone added in the order *e, f, g, h*

of the possible komis (4½, 5, 5½), and believe it or not the professionals adopt different strategies for each one, but komi for amateurs is usually 5 points in friendly games and 5½ in tournaments.

The idea of giving komi did not really catch on until after 1945; so if you play over games by the old masters remember that White is playing at a disadvantage. The top professional tournaments are now all played with komi, but at lower levels the professionals also use another rather complicated system based on the old method. For instance the weaker player may take Black in two games and White in one, with no komi. The reason for this is that the differences between the professional dan grades are much smaller than among amateurs. The top professional (9-dan) could give the lowest (sho-dan) only about 3 stones.

Just for reference, you will sometimes meet variations in handicaps. For example, instead of giving 2 stones White might give Black 10 points komi and first move. There is nothing wrong with this, but it is not usual.

A HANDICAP GAME

Handicap strategy is different, mainly because White is very cramped. White, to win, has to make more efficient use of his stones; he has to make fewer mistakes.

Black must remember that most or all of his handicap stones are on the fourth line. They are thus oriented towards the centre. A frequent mistake is for Black to try to seal off the corners, which contradicts the meaning of handicap stones.

The following game is a good example of well-played handicap Go—a simultaneous game played in New York in 1972. White is Ichigen Okubo, professional 9-dan. Black, with 7 stones handicap, is Mario Roberson, amateur 1-kyu.

Play this game over without worrying too much about the tactics. Try instead to follow the strategy. Black loses mainly because he tries to form side territories on the fourth line; they are a bit too exposed to White's encroachment. On the tactical level note at the end how Black has several clumps of stones, signifying inefficient plays, and how White usually manages to come away from each fight with sente.

Black doesn't make any serious mistakes till the very end, when he lets White play inside his bottom left corner group to produce seki. White could make it ko (see p.19) but he knows he has won anyway (by 6 points); so he is kind to Black.

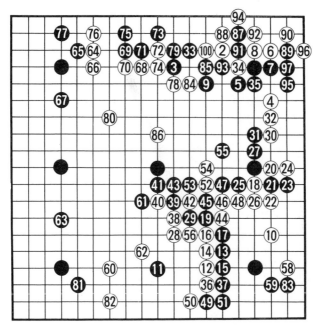

Diagram 120 (1—100)   57 connects at 42
98 takes two stones at 34
99 takes 98 at 91

The dame-filling sequence in this game requires some explanation. For instance, Black has to fill in at *b* because White can play at *a*. Strictly speaking moves like this should be played out, but players prefer to keep them as ko threats and treat them as dame. If you are not sure just play everything out. White cannot play at *c* until he has played at *d*. If he does play *c*, Black *d* (atari). White *e*, Black *f* captures 5 white stones in a snapback. *h* and *g*, and *i* and *j*, are similar to *a* and *b*; i.e. White plays one and Black must answer by connecting. Finally, when Black plays *k* White must play *l*, then Black *m*, White *n*; otherwise Black can capture the 10 white stones (it is a mistake to play White *k*). Note that dame inside a seki are never filled in.

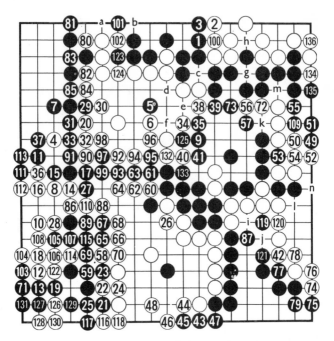

Diagram 121 (101—236)

10 Go throughout the world

The history of Go reputedly goes back about 4000 years to China, but actual records, including the oldest known game, go back only to A.D. 200 — still a considerable ancestry. Go was already well developed when it came to Japan some time around A.D. 550.

Originally one of the '4 sublime pastimes' of scholars, Go occupied a major place in China and Japan, being considered good for the mind—competence in Go was valued like a university degree—and useful to the military man. It is possible in fact to see the surrounding strategy of Go being applied in military campaigns in the Far East even today. (See, for example, *The Protracted Game: a Wei Ch'i Interpretation of Maoist Strategy* by Scott Borman (Oxford University Press 1969). Wei Ch'i is the Chinese name for Go.)

With such a reputation Go naturally attracted the patronage of the emperors, and in Japan it became the practice for aristocratic households to employ the top players. One of the Shoguns (military rulers) of Japan founded a Go Academy in 1603 and appointed the best player at the time as its head. This was Honinbo (pronounced and sometimes written Honimbo) Sansa.

Honinbo Sansa (who incidentally invented the dan and kyu system) had, like all the other Go masters, to spend much of his time teaching, and the tradition was for the best pupil to become his adopted son and to take the name of the master. Thus the family name of Honinbo was passed from generation to generation. Rivalry between this family and other illustrious Go families (Inoue, Yasui, Hayashi) has provided Go with a rich folklore and many famous games, but despite all the ups and downs the Honinbos reigned supreme. Strangely their hegemony was threatened most of all not by the other families but by the 'barbarians' from the West.

The most difficult time for all the Go professionals was the Meiji Restoration (1868 onwards), when for the first time Japan was opened up to the West, and in the excitement a number of the traditional ways were abandoned. Fortunately after some years a reaction set in, and early this century Go began to be fostered with even more zeal than before. Newspapers started to print Go articles and to sponsor major games. The enthusiasm has continued ever since.

The Nihon Kiin (Japan Go Association—something like a guild for professional players) was set up in 1924, and really came into its own during the war, when the 21st Honinbo, Shusai, announced that he was donating the family name to the Kiin so that professionals could compete annually for the honour of holding it. This was the start of tournament Go, and the first Honinbo-sen (*sen* = tournament) was held in 1941. (Shusai was immortalized in Kawabata's novel *Master of Go*.)

The coming of tournament Go also brought other reforms in its wake. One was the introduction of komi. Another was the drawing up for the first time of a code of rules for Go. This was in 1949 — only 4000 years late!

Surprisingly, despite this, there is still no set of rules which is entirely satisfactory. There are problems of logic to do with the end of the game and the rulings on the exceptional cases, but the Nihon Kiin rules are accepted everywhere except in China. The Chinese count differently, counting stones played as well as vacant points of territory. They also count points in a seki and play out situations like bent four in the corner. Reform of the rules is a permanent preoccupation in Japan and China, but nothing gets done, and most people seem quite happy to leave things as they are. Even the 19×19 board is not sacrosanct. For centuries a 17×17 board was used, and today professionals are experimenting with 21×21.

In China, Go did not flourish in the early part of this century as it did in Japan, although it was widely played. Since 1949, however, the game has been actively encouraged by the Communist Government. At the time of the rapprochement between Japan and China there was intense curiosity about how strong the Chinese players were, and a match was arranged. The Japanese professionals won, but got an awful fright.

In fact in Japan itself two of the top players are from Taiwan and Shanghai. One, Go Sei Gen, is particularly famous, together with the Japanese Minoru Kitani, for introducing the shin-fuseki. This was in the thirties, before tournament Go; so the pre-eminence of these players has unfortunately never been reflected in championship titles. The other, Rin Kai Ho, seemed to be running away with all the major titles in the early seventies until a young Japanese, Yoshio Ishida, bounced up from nowhere. This saviour of the Japanese national face, nicknamed 'The Computer' because of his powers of calculation in yose, seems to have an edge on Rin at the moment, but to make matters more interesting a young Korean, Cho Chi Kun, is shortly expected to reach the level of these two.

Those who make it to the top can do well financially. Every professional can make a basic though meagre living by playing in the Nihon Kiin's own permanent tournament, the Oteai. The top players can also win very substantial prizes in major tournaments sponsored by outside bodies such as the Press and Television.

The Honinbo-sen is the longest-running title, although not the richest. There are two honorary Honinbos. Takagawa (whose games are particularly rewarding to study because of their beautiful simplicity) won the title nine years in succession from 1952 to 1960; Sakata won seven times from 1961 to 1967, and has also won 51 major tournaments — far more than anybody else. Since then the title has been contested between the young men Ishida and Rin.

The richest tournament is the *Meijin-sen*. This started in 1962, and Rin has come nearest to monopolizing it. Meijin is the most coveted title. Like Honinbo it was granted to the Kiin by its last holder Shusai. Of the others the *10-dan tournament* (this is only a title, not a permanent promotion), the *Pro Best Ten*, and *Oza-sen* attract the most attention. The Oza is dominated by the older players because they can still cope with its time-limit of six hours each. The ten hours each of the other tournaments seems to be too tiring for the veterans.

The games in these tournaments are reported daily in the national press, and there is also a special lightning tournament (half an hour a game) on television. Go columns appear in a wide variety of journals—even women's magazines: there are several good lady professionals. Many Go clubs in Japan are run on a commercial basis, and companies also have their own clubs. The company frequently pays for a couple of professionals to come weekly and give lessons. What ultimately justifies all this Go activity is the fact that there are about ten million players in Japan (served by about 500 professionals).

As a result of all this coverage it is hardly surprising that the standard amongst Japanese amateurs is very high indeed. Some of the top amateurs can, in fact, easily beat the lesser professionals, but many are semi-professional themselves, writing Go columns and ghosting books for the 'pros'. The professionals can earn a good deal of money not only from tournaments and books but also from television appearances and from endorsing advertisements for whisky, hair cream, and so on.

And where is the West in all this? Well, in 1975 the first non-Oriental professionals came on the scene. Actually they are *insei* (student professionals) at the moment. One is an American, James Kerwin; the other an Austrian, Manfred Wimmer; but of course if they want to make a living out of Go they will have to study, and probably play, in Japan.

Outside Japan there are professionals in Korea, and semi-professionals in China, but the players in Europe and North and South America are all amateurs. Most cities in Europe and the USA have Go clubs. London even has a Go Centre which opens seven days a week (see photograph on page 76). Every country has its own Go Association (p.85) which organizes national tournaments, keeps a register of players, supervises gradings, and so on.

There is also a European Go Federation which has been in existence for over 20 years. Their major event is the annual European Championship, an event dominated by the Germans, although an Austrian and a Yugoslav

*The author (2-dan) losing gallantly to Machiko Inoue (professional showdan)
at the London Go Centre*

have won in recent years. The present champion is Jürgen Mattern, 6-dan
from Germany. (For comparison the top British player is 5-dan, the top
American 6-dan).

People in the West starting the game now are extremely lucky by comparison with those who began a few years ago. Until recently there was
virtually no English literature available. Now there are publishing firms
specializing in English Go books, and the problem is one of choice. A similar
story applies to Go equipment.

Furthermore we now have frequent access to the professionals; parties
come over from Japan several times a year, travelling round Europe and
America playing simultaneous games and giving lectures. The photograph
above shows one such occasion.

One thing we still lack, however, is our own terminology for the game.
We use the Japanese terms all the time, even if a satisfactory English
equivalent exists. This is perhaps a legacy of days when players had to
struggle through Japanese books to make any progress, and it may change
in time. The French at least have made a start. They call a long line of
stones by the apt name *baguette*. The idea of a loaf of bread on the Go
board sounds most appealing. You may be part of the new generation of
Go players that will anglicize the game's terminology in the same way — let
us hope with the same panache.

11 A professional game

Since you were subjected to an example of the worst kind of play in Chapter 4, it seems only right that you should also see some of the best. This of course means a professional game.

You must understand that at this level Go is no longer just a game. It is a medium for creating things of beauty, even once in a while for creating art.

This is not as pretentious as it sounds to Western ears. We should at least try to appreciate first of all the place in Japanese society which Go holds and has held for 400 years. The ten million regular players are not mere followers of fashion, and Go is not simply a social accomplishment. It is in fact a kind of safety valve by which the tensions of everyday life can be relieved. People who must at all times be on their guard to observe the minutest distinctions of class can, over the Go board, assume the guise of the ronin, the wandering samurai who owes allegiance to no one, the warrior who knows no fear.

The fighting spirit of those players at the top must therefore be second to none. And lest they forget, all round them are reminders of a past filled with illustrious Go warriors who staked their lives on games.

They must also be masters of their craft. Behind even the youngest champion will lie an apprenticeship of twenty years' hard work, and once at the top nobody can afford to relax or coast along. The hard work goes on and on.

The expectations of the public are built up even more by newspapers and television. Every single move is under the scrutiny of expert commentators, who are addressing an informed audience, and beware those professionals whose moves are criticized for lack of fighting spirit.

On the other hand the conditions for top-level games are made conducive to producing the very best Go. A game like the one on the following pages, the final of a major championship sponsored by a leading newspaper, takes place in idyllic surroundings, perhaps in a Japanese-style inn in a mountain resort. The equipment they use, costing maybe £10 000, is so exquisitely designed that it becomes unthinkable for anyone to sully it with inferior moves.

During the game the players are sealed off from the rest of the world, and nothing is allowed to interfere with their state of mind. For two days they are locked in combat, ten hours a day.

This is the atmosphere that leads to a constant striving for perfection, and it is this in turn that leads eventually to art.

The game that follows was played in the final of the 27th Honinbo-Sen.

A professional game

Ishida was already Honinbo; his opponent was Rin Kai Ho, at that time
Meijin. For the two players, this final was to decide who was the champion
of champions; for the public, Ishida was on trial to save the honour of
Japan.

From the purely technical point of view games between these two
players are always absorbing. They are difficult to understand, although
presumably even the other professionals find this so! But Ishida's style is
particularly interesting because he makes moves at which other professionals would laugh if they were made by amateurs. Ishida in fact is
humble enough to borrow ideas from amateur players — and improve them,
of course. His style in general is to grab territory early on and to rely on
his fighting ability to stop his opponent getting the centre. He is also considered to be the game's best yose player, from which comes his nickname
of 'The Computer'.

Ishida is very popular in Japan, but surprisingly perhaps so is Rin. He is
Chinese, but he came to Japan at a very early age to study Go, and has
won enormous respect for his achievements. Apart from Sakata, and just
recently Ishida, he is the only player to have held the Honinbo and Meijin
titles simultaneously, something which the Japanese regard as particularly
mind-boggling.

Rin's style is more conservative than Ishida's, and he seems to be happy
in almost any type of game. Like the other famous Chinese player, Go Sei
Gen, he is far less aggressive than the Japanese.

You will see both styles exemplified here. This is a fairly straightforward
game, chosen in the hope that you will find it reasonably easy to follow.
Highly detailed notes would be pointless; comments are made only about
some general themes that you have seen already (such as sente and aji), and
ideas you can reasonably expect to pick up yourself from professional games,
once you know what to look for.

You can assume, by the way, that professionals do not make mistakes.
They may make one or two in a game, but in many cases you have to be a
professional yourself to understand why it was a mistake. In other words,
anything you pick up from these games, use!

The theme of this game is that both players try to stake out large territories. Black feels worried about his opponent's large *moyo*, and plays inside his territory to reduce it. (Note the light, flexible way he does so). White
counter-attacks this group. As so often happens the weak group can live
easily, but the fighting spills over into other areas occupied by Black, in
this case the top right corner. Because of the ferocity of the attack on this
corner Black has to give something up, either part of the corner or part of
his centre group. He chooses the latter. Black already has more secure
territory than White; so this loss makes the game very close.

One thing you should try to imitate is the way these players seal off

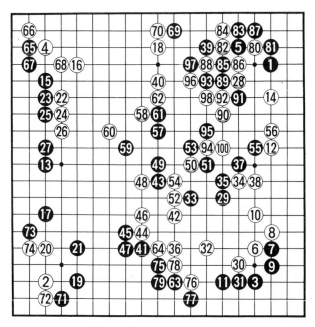

Diagram 122 (1—100)   Rin Kai Ho v. Yoshio Ishida
Honinbo-sen 1972
(4½ points komi)
99 connects at 88

large territories. This is something amateur players find very difficult. The best way is to do it by attacking the opponent, so that he has no time to invade or reduce the territory you are forming. Note how White in this game sealed off his territory at the top on the side facing the centre. This is the easiest one to follow. You can see the same thing for the white area on the right and the black territory at the bottom but these are less easy to follow.

Finally try to play this game several times. You will not only get more out of it this way, you will also be able to judge your progress by seeing how much more of it you understand each time.

White 4: This was the first time the double san-san arrangement of 2 and 4 had been played in a major tournament. It has since become very popular with amateurs and professionals alike. It had previously been thought that these moves were too 'low', and made it too hard for White to contest the centre. This game explodes that idea.

A professional game

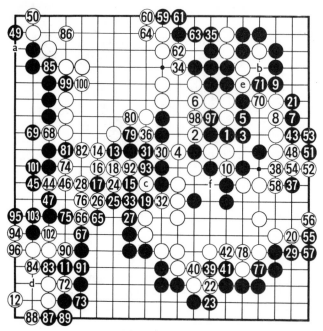

Diagram 123 (101—203) a to f are *dame*

White 12: This is the end of the end of the only joseki in this game, in the bottom right corner. Compare the development of this in the final position with the development of the same joseki in the game in Chapter 7. White 28: This is always a vital point of the shimari, for both players.

Black 29: The simple way to play is at 32, but this is too slow. It would start to seal off the bottom edge, but it would allow White more time to seal off the even bigger right side. Remember the komi too. This 29 is the start of a new black group in the centre designed to reduce White's territory.

Black 41: One of the functions of this move is to help stones 19 and 21, in case they should be cut off from the left side group.

White 50: An eye-stealing move.

White 58—60: Making territory while attacking.

Black 65: A very early start to yose, played only because it was sente and because the other side of this territory is now settled by 57 to 61, so there is no reason to keep any aji here.

White 82: The start of a vicious attack that Black had not foreseen. The corner is quite safe, but the purpose behind White's moves is to build up a position here so that he can attack the still-weak centre group more strongly. Note in particular White 90. There are very many possible vari-

80

ations here, most of them 30-50 moves long. Suffice it to say that both players have worked them all out.

White 112: The right shape to get two eyes.

White 120: Back to yose. This is better than continuing to attack in the centre. The attack might end in gote and then Black would get all the yose points.

Black 139—141. Note that the order of these moves is very important. If they are reversed White will ignore the second black move and take sente, which is worth more than the two stones he is sacrificing.

White 144: Again note how sente comes before gote at 148.

The rest of the game is yose, and uneventful, but Rin was short of time, after thinking for a very long time over 82, and he may have lost one or two points at this stage.

The game ended at move 203. Ishida won by 1½ points (after allowing for komi). He went on to win the series of seven games which make up the final, and thus retained his Honinbo title.

Appendix   The rules of Go

Players   Two; one takes the black stones and one the white.

Moves   Black plays first. The players then take turns to place a new
stone at any vacant intersection on the board (including the edges),
subject only to the prohibitions of ko and suicide. A player may
pass at any time.
Once played the stones cannot be moved.

Capture   Stones whose liberties are completely filled in by the
opponent's stones are captured and removed from the board immediately. If there are any stones that cannot avoid capture at the
end of the game (i.e. dead stones) they are removed at the end of
the game and count as captured stones. It is not then necessary to
fill in the liberties of these stones.

Suicide   No stone can be played into a position of immediate capture
unless this move immediately captures one or more of the opponent's
stones.

Ko   It is not permissible to play a move which would leave the position
exactly the same as before the move the opponent has just played.

Object   The object of the game is to get more points than the opponent,
either by forming territories (i.e. surrounded areas of vacant intersections) or by capturing the opponent's stones.

End   The game ends when there are two consecutive passes, or if both
players agree. Counting then begins.

Counting   Each player counts 1 point for every vacant intersection he
has surrounded with his own stones in the final position with all
captured and dead stones removed. He also counts 1 point for every
stone he has captured during the game, including dead stones.

Exceptions   Bent four in the corner is dead.
No points are counted inside a seki.
For other unusual positions see Chapter 8.

Index of Go technical terms

The following list contains the technical terms used in this book, in which case they are followed by a page reference, and also those terms that most English-speaking players actively use. All foreign words are Japanese, but their pronunciation suffers the mutilation typical of English speakers. Final 'e' is pronounced 'ay' as in 'say'.

aji: 58
aji keshi: a move or sequence that
    removes aji is said to be aji keshi.
alive: 15
atari: 8

bamboo joint: 35
bent four in the corner: 40
block: 30
byoyomi: 55

capturing: 7
connection: 7
cross-cut: the position shown at A in
    Diagram 124 where each player's
    stones cut the other's into two
    groups.

dame: 12, 71
damezumari: 33
dan: 3
dead: 15
dead stones: 9
direct ko: 63
double ko: 64

empty triangle: the position shown at
    B in Diagram 124; regarded as in-
    efficient shape and to be avoided.
eternal life: 66
eye: 15

false eye: 16
furikawari: 53
fuseki: 48

geta: 30
gote: 56

handicaps: 68
hane: the small upward flourish at the
    end of a vertical stroke in Chinese
    writing is called *hane*; in Go it
    refers to a move where you bend
    round your opponent's stones
    from a straight line of your own
    stones but at an angle of 45° to
    your stones: e.g. move 1 in Dia-
    gram 124.
Honinbo: 73
horikomi: 33
hoshi: 53

indirect ko: 63
insei: 75

jigo: 68
joseki: 48, 53

kakari: 53
katachi: 'shape', but always used to
    mean good shape, referring to any
    local arrangement of stones that
    is efficient. An empty triangle is
    an example of bad shape.
keima: the arrangement of stones 2
    and Ⓐ in Diagram 124, this being
    a representation of the knight's
    move in chess.
ko: 10
komi: 68
komoku: 53
kosumi: a diagonal extension from a
    stone of the same colour but with
    no space in between; e.g. move 3
    in Diagram 124.
kyu: 3

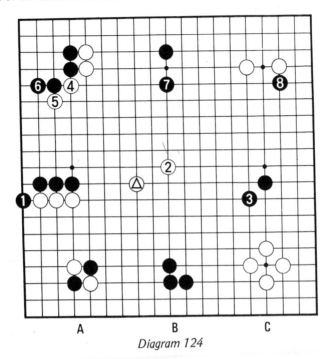

Diagram 124

semeai: (pronounced 'semi-eye') a
position in which a black group
and a white group do not have
two eyes and can get life only by
killing the other group. Both
players race to fill in the liberties
of the opposing group first.
sente: 56
shicho: 31
shimari: 53
shin-fuseki: 48
shodan: 3
snapback: 33
star points: 2
suicide: 9
sute ishi: 34

taisha: 54
takamoku: 53
tengen: 49
10 000 year ko: 66
territory: 6
tesuji: 34
throw-in: 26

tobi: a 'jump'; i.e. a move at least one
point away from a friendly stone
in a vertical or horizontal direction.
A one-point jump, called *ikken
tobi*, is shown by move 7 in
Diagram 124.
triple ko: 65
tsuke: 'attachment'; a move such as
8 in Diagram 124 where a single
stone is played directly against an
enemy group.
tsume go: problems, usually small
corner or side positions, in which
you have to find the right sequence
to ensure life, death or ko.
two eyes: 14

uttegaeshi: 33

wall: 5

yose: 61
yose-ko: 64
yosu miru: 59

GO ASSOCIATIONS

British Go Association
Go Advisory Service
8 Hanover Street
London
W1R 0DR

American Go Association
P.O. Box 397
Old Chelsea Station
New York 10011
U.S.A.

These bodies will supply addresses of other national Go associations.

EQUIPMENT AND BOOKS

Inexpensive Go equipment is available in most toy shops. Top-quality
equipment is available in many cities, but expert advice should be taken
before buying. The national Go associations usually supply equipment
and books, but the most comprehensive selections are provided by the
following, who can also deal with trade enquiries:

London Go Centre
18 Lambolle Place
London NW3 4RG
U.K.

Tokyo Sales Corporation
142 West 57th Street
New York 10019
U.S.A.

Ishi Press Inc.
CPO Box 2126
Tokyo
Japan